77808

Faith and Community

Faith and Community

A Christian

Existential Approach

by

CLYDE A. HOLBROOK

HARPER & BROTHERS PUBLISHERS

NEW YORK

Library of Congress catalog card number: 59-7153

To Dorothy, Richard, Arthur and Deborah:
to the influence of each, these pages testify

Contents

Preface

THIS book contains a series of essays which explore the meaning of faith and its moral implications. My basic purpose has been to spell out, as coherently as possible, my own understanding of faith. It has not been my intention to pose as one who lays down authoritative and universally valid prescriptions as to how others have experienced or will experience faith. I have not undertaken to speak on behalf of Christianity, Protestantism, the Church, or that type of existentialism which in many ways stands close to Biblical insights. Rather, I have carried on an internal dialogue with many viewpoints and with myself, the end result of which is here presented, for the most part, in a "confessional" tone. I have attempted to say to the reader: "This is what faith means to me. Look now at your existence in the light of these perspectives, and then decide for yourself what meaning faith has in your life." The author does not presume to deprive the reader of his freedom to come to his own decision in an area where personal decision is crucial.

Although an inevitably personal note runs through these essays, I have laid under tribute the insights of many who have stimulated and enriched my thought. The influences of Paul and the Reformers, Augustine and Kierkegaard, H. R. Niebuhr and Buber, Whitehead and Jaspers, Brunner and Bultmann, E. P. Dickie and Tillich, among many others, are not difficult to trace out. These pages would be immeasurably impoverished without their contributions. Yet of none of these men have I consciously been a slavish disciple. Even as I cannot substitute my judgments for those of the reader, neither can I permit these authors to stand in my stead or to share the slightest blame for any improper use to which I have put their reflections.

As one of the purposes of this introduction is to acquaint the reader with the terrain over which I propose to guide him, I should point out the general plan and content of the book. At the outset two forms of faith are distinguished from each other: primal and radical. The first is the inevitable condition in which all men live by virtue of being finite creatures. The second is the possibility in which men may live by virtue of being sinners. We awake, as it were, to find ourselves in primal faith, whereas radical faith involves decisions and commitment of a more or less conscious type. Of course, there are other views of faith, some of which are critically examined in the second chapter for the purpose of clarifying the character of radical faith understood as a mode of existence rather than as a means of knowing God. In Christianity the supreme agent through whom radical faith lays hold upon its ultimate object is Jesus Christ. In the light of the New Testament the meaning of Christ for faith is explored next, in order to show the unique nature of Christian faith. The ultimate object for Christian faith is God, and some of the ways in which man and God meet are described in the final chapter of the first section of the book.

The second section takes up the ethical question as it has been dealt with in several historical perspectives. It evaluates these alternative readings of ethics and discusses the transformation of the ethical problem itself in the light of Christian faith. The concluding chapter is an exposition of the ethic of community and reconciliation as the outworking of the faith relation in which the Christian stands.

Henry Adams once remarked, "No man means all he says, and yet very few say all they mean, for words are slippery and thought is viscous."[1] Perhaps nowhere is the truth of this comment more easily recognizable than when one attempts to translate states of vibrant and dynamic existence into the pallid forms of verbal communication. The reader himself must retranslate what is written here into that secret interior language of the self which alone proves faithful to his personal existence.

This book was completed while I was residing at the universities of St. Andrews and Basel. For the opportunity of enjoying the hospitality and intellectual stimulation of these ancient seats of learning, I am grateful to the Danforth Foundation as well as to the institutions themselves. My thanks are tendered to the distinguished faculty of St. Mary's College, St. Andrews University, for its cordial reception and many favors. Its members have placed me so deeply in their debt that I fear these few words must be regarded as a mere token discharge of my obligation to them. Behind these pages, yet more intimately linked with them than they would admit, stand the Rev. William J. McCullough and Dean Rayborn L. Zerby. Without their faith and insight I would probably never have begun to think about the issues raised in this book. My wife and children have stood up remarkably well under the tribulations of my authorship. To them I dedicate the results of my work as a partial repayment for more hours of enforced silence and exile from the paternal presence than I care to count.

CLYDE A. HOLBROOK

Oberlin College
January, 1959

Part One

Faith and Personal Existence

I

Primal Faith and Radical Faith

Now faith is the assurance of things hoped for, the conviction of things not seen. [Hebrews 11:1]

But we have this treasure in earthen vessels, to show that the transcendent power belongs to God and not to us. We are afflicted in every way, but not crushed; perplexed, but not driven to despair; persecuted, but not forsaken; struck down, but not destroyed. [II Corinthians 4:7-9]

> Whither shall I go from thy spirit?
> Or whither shall I flee from thy presence?
> If I ascend to heaven, thou art there!
> If I make my bed in Sheol, thou art there!
> [Psalm 139:7-8]

And Jesus said to him, "If you can! All things are possible to him who believes." Immediately the father of the child cried out and said, "I believe; help my unbelief!" [Mark 9:23-24]

WE ALL live in the condition of faith, for faith in its elementary form is not an appendage to life but the inevitable form our existence takes, because we are in the deepest sense contingent and dependent creatures. Deeper than all distinctions of race, class, religion, or personal endowments lies the unity we have as personal beings. And this unity in large part consists of our being together in a universe upon whose intricate and subtle operations at all levels we depend absolutely. We live in faith because there is no other way in which to live.

For many of us this inevitability of faith is difficult to recognize. It is so intimately interwoven into our lives that it escapes notice in the press of more obvious experiences. Bergson was right when he commented, "That which is immediate is far from being that which is the easiest to perceive."[1] Cassius inquires, "Tell me, good Brutus, can you see your face?" to which Brutus replies, "No, Cassius, for the eye sees not itself, But by reflection, by some other things."[2] So it is with much of our experience. What is most intimately and necessarily involved in our existence may be the last thing which we appreciate. We do not see our eyes, smell our noses, hear our ears, or think our brains. They come to the forefront of consciousness either by some reflexive act of the mind or by the shock of injury and disease. When that happens, we are suddenly made aware of what complete and unquestioning trust we have vested in these organs and their functions, yet how fully they have been incorporated into ourselves and hidden within what we call "normal" experience.

When, in a preliminary way, we turn to examine faith, a similar principle holds: what is primary in existence often comes last in thought and consciousness. Thus, to grasp faith we must adopt the strategy of the reflexive act. We must attempt to frame a question in such a way as to bring to the surface what we sense dimly to lie in the depth. We turn back upon ourselves as concretely existing persons to glimpse what is taking place "behind the scenes," and then attempt to draw out the implications and consequences of that hidden existence.

The most productive query, perhaps, with which to set out might be stated in either of two forms: "What must I absolutely presuppose in order to account for the totality of my existence, as best I know it?" Or "What have I accepted, consciously or unconsciously, into the very fabric of my being, as the absolute ground of my life?" It is clear that what we seek is not a scheme of "ideas" or "beliefs" but rather the vibrant realities, the actualities to which such ideas or beliefs may point. We are not seeking theoretical constructs but the nature of whatever existence makes possible and understandable the range of our lives. It should also be manifest that the dynamic character of our personal existence and the proximity to ourselves of these supposed actualities rule out the possibility of a complete answer to our questions. We may be able to answer only in part, yet even that part may illuminate the character of the faith to which we have referred.

What then do we discover about faith when we attempt this reflexive approach? First we find that we are in the midst, not at the beginning, of living. By the time we become conscious of ourselves as selves, we realize, a great deal of experience has already gone into our making. We have been eating, drinking, deciding between this and that prized object, loving, hating, hoping, all the time cradled by ignorance or lack of conscious effort and choice. In a highly complex way we have been accepting and giving assent, by our mental and physical actions, to ourselves, to other persons, and to the world about us. Yet so far as we can press our scrutiny into the past or present, there never was a time when we first decided to commit ourselves thus. With birth, if not before, we put down the full weight of our fragile lives upon physical, psychological, social, and rational processes of which we apparently had not the slightest comprehension. In a naïve but absolute fashion we commenced and went on living, without any rational determination to do so. Our dependence was attested by what we did, not by what we thought or decided. We accepted and trusted because that was the only way to exist. Such "faith" is the prerequisite to existence of any kind. It is given with existence itself; it is the tribute which must be paid to unconditional dependence.[3] By the time we embark on the reflexive inquiry, it is too late either to begin afresh on a more rational foundation for our lives or to deny our rootage in this primal faith. Personal identity and autonomy arise in the matrix of faith, with its unspoken but enacted pledges, but they cannot disown their parentage. We awake to discover ourselves caught in this faith, which we have chosen to designate as "elemental" or "primal" to distinguish it from the faith of decision, which we call "radical" faith.[4]

To some extent we can sketch the nature of elemental faith. Our biological nature, as well as the physical world of which it forms a part, is not produced by human ingenuity and skill. We receive it from beyond ourselves. It is a "given" in which human calculation or choice plays no part. We may in certain relatively minor ways modify physical nature, but to do so we must first accept it as fact. Our action of modification attests the prior reality of both the modifier and that which is modified. We depend completely, not hypothetically, upon our physical functions and the relative constancy of nature by which they are organized and sustained.[5] By our daily actions we proclaim our trust in them more loudly than any argument can possibly do.

In a like manner our psychological capabilities are accepted from beyond ourselves and form part of the basal substance out of which we live. We remember, will, think, feel, and sense, and thereby make possible communication, knowledge, and the delicate fabric of culture. Yet, in spite of the greater freedom and adaptability which our psychological nature provides, we are still totally dependent upon it. We may doubt our senses or reason; we may be subject to hallucinations and neuroses, but these occur by virtue of an intricate psychological structure without which we would not be human in any clear sense. Our reason forms no small part of this aspect of our natures, but again, even when we doubt by means of our reason, we affirm our dependence upon it in a most uncompromising fashion. We may doubt our doubts; we may not doubt so radically that the existence of reason itself is put in jeopardy. It is an integral actuality of the self.[6]

Our social nature is also given to us in the fact of our existence. By no deliberative choice on our part, we discover ourselves remarkably dependent upon other persons and the institutions of society. To be a self is to be a social self in such a way that we give pledges of ourselves to others from the moment we begin to live. Our individual existence presupposes society. We have to make a choice to withdraw from society; we do not make a choice to be in and of society. The recluse, the hermit, the celibate takes with him in memory, if in no other way, the social nexus which made him and from which he rebels. He must affirm himself against society because that is the prior condition of his existence which he did not have to choose.

In these three areas—physical, psychological, and social—we find that we adopt no tentative or hypothetical attitude. We accept them as constitutive of our existence. We are committed to them, albeit usually unconsciously, yet with such abiding power that whatever ideas and speculations we entertain about them in retrospect, we never in fact deny them. They form the tacit presuppositions or realities of our existence. They form the inescapable substance, accepted into the essence of our lives. This acceptance, on which our lives are based, we call primal faith. Neither irrational nor rational in character, this faith is the primordial source of our personal existence.

However, our original question must reach further. We have uncovered what is absolutely presupposed within human existence,

but of course we have not yet come to the more profound issues involved in a single person's existence, in "my" existence—and that is a more productive area of inquiry.

Retaining the original question concerning what I presuppose absolutely for my existence, we must now supplement it with another query: "What does it mean to live as a person caught up in this situation of complete trust and absolute dependence? What is my individual significance as one who is inevitably in faith?" The testimony of this particular self must be heard: the testimony of one who is not simply an example of a higher mammal, a psychological instance, or a segment of society.

When we put this supplementary question, we recognize at once that no general answer will satisfy it, for the question is one which isolates us, forces us into the open as separate persons. Each must give his own response. Because this particular, unique self has never lived before, or if so, has no ready recollection of his past, he finds, in Kierkegaard's words, that there are "no answers in the back of the book." I must venture to answer for myself with whatever hazards are involved.

I may find helpful insights for my answer in poetry, music, philosophy, religion, and science, but the final word awaits my decision. I may live a while in the light of increasing information, but it comes to definite result only by some decisive act of my own. The restless urge for my own personal meaning will at last drive me out of the comfort which information in general offers. I continue, in spite of all organized knowledge, to know myself as a contingent, unique person, somehow cast up on the shores of rational consciousness by the chancy tides of uncomprehended forces. From the mystery of myself I have no door of escape.

The use of the word "mystery" is not simply another way of expressing the conviction that life is filled with problems.[7] Problems can be formulated with some degree of specificity and stated in general terms. Various methods of resolution may be offered which again can be understood, criticized, used, or cast aside. Problems exist in the common world of discourse. Mystery, on the other hand, is personal and bespeaks involvement of the self in wonder, awe, and amazement in the presence of finitude. No increase of information eliminates mystery, for there remains the mystery of there being a self who can know. Knowledge takes place within our existence, and mystery attaches to existence itself. We begin

to be before we know why we are. And throughout life we run this race in which our being, our forward movement of existing, outspeeds the verdicts of reason. Growth in knowledge illuminates our existence; it enables us to peer into the future. But it also enlarges the field of mystery because wonder attaches to the knowledge itself. At last we must face, as a matter of responsible decision, what it means to us personally to live in a world where we do not hold in our hands either the source or the destiny of history—our own or others'.

Yet mystery is not identical with ignorance. As Hocking has pointed out, "Religion is bound up in the difference between the the sense of ignorance and the sense of mystery; the former means, 'I know not'; the latter means, 'I know not, but it is known' . . . The negative side is made possible by some prior recognition of a positive being on the other side of limitation."[8] Without some intimation of a power lurking on the other side of mystery, the clue of intelligibility disappears, and with it the mystery itself. We have no mystery if there is no reality beyond it by virtue of which it appears as a mystery.

At least two rather modest clues may be suggested. The first is that I am inescapably bound to ask the question of my own meaning in such a way that the answer to it must be one of concrete fulfillment of the self, rather than a series of ideas or a "life philosophy." I find I do not and cannot simply take life as it comes. I press insatiably for that which in some sense satisfies my being as a whole, not only as a rational self. I find myself irresistibly lured on by a meaning which shall at last be an event, not merely an idea made the object of contemplation. Indeed, even when I vigorously proclaim in moments of greatest stress that I and my world are totally devoid of meaning, namely, that I and the world are sufficiently meaningful to be understood as having no meaning, I cannot twist away from the notion of fulfillment and significance. By virtue of living at all we are pointed toward meaning.

Sometimes it is said that a suicide has lost faith, and with that loss, meaning has disappeared from his life. But is this the case? Suicide may be the frantic and misguided attempt to break away from all that frustrates the self's quest for significance, but it is never a final denial of faith or meaning as such. It is rather the transposition of faith into a disharmonious, self-destructive mode by which it is still anticipated in another realm, or by the dramatic act itself, to fulfill meaning. As Jaspers sees it, "There is no tragedy without

transcendence. Even defiance unto death in a hopeless battle against gods and fate is an act of transcendency; it is a movement towards man's proper essence, which he comes to know as his own in the presence of his doom."[9] In the effort to rise above "fate," the self clings to the hope of its final salvation. Faith is represented by the inviolable attachment which each self has to the quest for fulfillment. The most bedeviled soul is caught up in an implicit orientation toward meaning which his agonized attempt at nonexistence does not fundamentally dispute. His claim to be valued may be rejected by disease, intolerable cruelty, evil habits, indifference, or betrayal, but the self persists in claiming its value, if not "here," then "there."

"If a man cannot justify himself in his happiness and his success," wrote Dietrich Bonhoeffer, one who knew whereof he spoke, "he can still justify himself in his despair. . . . Suicide is a man's attempt to give final human meaning to a life which has become humanly meaningless."[10] In some moment of heroic splendor, stoical courage, or demonic afflatus, perhaps unseen and unshared by any other, the despairing one seeks self-understanding and self-justification in the act by which he believes the secret is unraveled, the elusive meaning conferred. And each of us in more normal circumstances is no less bound to this search for fulfillment than is the pitiable suicide.

The second clue follows hard upon the first. Wherever we pursue this inevitable search for our meaning, it becomes clear that the answer does not lie simply locked up within the self. Even as my existence is "given" from beyond myself, so also the quest for meaning and its fulfillment are "given" to me. "If a man is to find himself," C. A. Bennett declared, "he must first find in the world outside some power that is either friend or foe,"[11] which is to say that no amount of inward contemplation reveals to me my significance; I can but descend deeper and deeper into a chaos of feelings and embryonic ideas.

If I seek to coil about me my personal satisfactions and pleasures, if I adopt the pose of stoic indifference, my personal insufficiency only appears the more strikingly. If I immerse myself in music, art, sensuality, power, or religion, I discover at last that I am not as a total person fulfilled; I have only lost myself and avoided the quest for my significance by sacrificing myself to that which did not create me a person. I cannot secure ultimate significance by attaching myself to that which is as finite and contingent as I myself am.

What I have is a thirst for a reality which is adequate to my total condition, the encounter with a reality so indubitable that I can in full consciousness give myself to it. For this I must move outside the orbit of the self and all that can conceivably be construed to depend upon it. I must come to that which is the all-embracing source of both being and value, God Himself. When I recognize that this is my true situation, I then also know that my absolute dependence is not upon merely the physical, psychological, and social but upon that by virtue of which these exist. Faith has been all the time the silent witness to the bond which finally draws me back to be fulfilled in Him by virtue of whom I live.

If it is possible then to become aware of One there in the dark, however dimly He is apprehended, why can we not press on to a fulfillment of meaning in Him? If existence is "given" existence, why do we not know the "giver"? If, in the last analysis, everyone does live, think, and act in such absolute dependence upon this mysterious source of being and value, why should we not be able to penetrate its secret?

Two answers to these queries may be ventured. The first, already suggested by our brief analysis of dependence and faith, is human finitude; the second is sin.

Our finitude is recognized not only in our dependence but by the definite limitations we soon become aware of as we begin to explore our world. There are inexorable limitations laid upon us by space and time, climate, geographical location, place of origin, structures of body and mind, cultural conditions, and the like. Some of these are more elastic to man's scientific control than others, but none of them seems subject to elimination. To have being apparently means to have some definite form of being, and a definite form of being, at least in our world of experience, involves limitation of possibilities —in short, finitude.

There are certain marks of finitude, however, which touch our consciousness with more than passing interest, and among these are guilt, suffering, the irreversible character of our personal histories, and death.[12] Such limitations are not external to us but caught up into the essence of our lives. We may storm them and destroy them in imagination, but in soberer moments we know we have only been thrown back, exhausted and spent. The limitations have been entangled in the very efforts for freedom. We do not transcend our finitudes; we do not succeed in debating them out of existence; they penetrate our whole being. And with the recognition of finitude life may take on a more serious or tragic flavor.

Death is one of the most impressive evidences of our finitude, so let us examine the possible impact which serious awareness of it may bring.

Everybody dies, and everybody knows it! But who is this "everybody" that dies? Is it only those whose names are found in the obituary column or marked on gravestones? Is it those people who now jostle each other at the bargain counter or in the theater lobby? Yes, we say it is "they," the anonymous ones, the masses who die.

But what if we face up to the fact that we too are among the "they"? What if I confront as fully as I may the fact that this "I" must cease to be? Now it is my limitation which I meet, and no statistical table or biological considerations will comfort me. Death is the end of my existence as I have known it, and with its coming all my plans stop in mid-air, all I cherish and love is lost, and, most poignant of all, I must face this prospect in isolation. No deeds I have performed, no cause exuberantly embraced, grant me respite from death's intrusion. Every man must die for himself, as Luther said, for death is the great individualizer. It does not issue a collective summons.

In much of Western culture we have been taught that these notions are morbid, and we have been given advice to rally from such distressing preoccupations. Consolations and explanations spring up to defend us from the distasteful consideration of our finitude. Pseudoscientific groups flourish which tell us they are on the way to conquering death. We delay death by promoting health conditions. We arrange patterns for our funerals so that there will be a minimal consideration of our own end. Whatever the future holds, however, the fact of death for each of us obtrudes.

We may say to ourselves, "I am an immortal soul bearing the image of God; therefore I, the real I, will not cease to be." "God is too good and wise to destroy his highest creation, human personality —and me in particular." Or "Death is a release from suffering and pain. It is a divine or natural mercy." "It would be an irrational universe if a few particles of dislocated matter snuffed out the value of sweet and gentle spirits I have known." Perhaps we take what we assume to be a more realistic attitude: "When it comes, it comes. When it is over, it is finished. So why worry?"

Yet there is something hollow and unconvincing in these words of comfort or indifference. How can we be so sure that we are worthy of continued personal existence, that God's goodness is of so soft a stuff that it cannot abide the destruction of His creation, that the universe is so remarkably rational that it is solicitous over one relatively insignificant individual? In the kind of world I see about me, reassuring answers are hard to come by. A trip through a natural history museum may set off some exceedingly long thoughts. A child dying of cancer, a native of central Africa felled by a tropical disease, or a woman dying in childbirth does not suggest a loving Father or a rational universe. Even when we greet death as merciful release from suffering, we know we are settling for a poor second best to what might have been, had there been no suffering in the first place. All talk of producing high character through suffering stumbles on the disproportion between the amount of suffering inflicted and the amount of character produced. Nor can we, on the other hand, let off lightly the cynic with his forced bravado about death's coming. Is he sure that death is the end? What if he has an eternity to spend with himself? Will his seeming "realism" desert him, not simply at the moment of physical death, but as he contemplates the coming of that moment? Does his bravado do more than underscore the fact that death is the enemy of life and that he has to meet it some way or other, yet not with calm acceptance of it as part of life? In every case, death comes, and to this our consolations and explanations are no more than temporary expedients.

We cannot think or feel as those who are certainly immortal. Over every project and fair hope the dread prospect lowers. Over every pretension to intellectual certainty, prestige, and virtue a stern pronouncement has been passed. The Caesars and Hitlers pass, as do the humblest slaves. The Platos and Hegels complete themselves in dying, as do the stupid and brutish. There is no advice in circular form to be handed out, telling us as individuals how we should die. All reports offered come from this side of the grave, from the situation of limit itself. No priestly incantation, no ghostly message from "another world" can save us from dying for ourselves. Death is the sentinel for whom we have no password.

There is a subtler aspect to the limitation of death, for death is not only physical cessation of being; it is a threat of nonexistence, which gnaws at every creative act of man's life. It does not come, as it were, at the end of life; it is an ingredient in the living itself. Heidegger sternly reminds us, "As soon as we are born, we are old enough to die."[13] There is the constant "dying" from youth to age, the sliding back into nonentity of what we labor to preserve, and man can sense this struggle of being against nonbeing within himself as long as life goes on. So Paul Tillich is moved to regard death not merely as "the scissors which cuts the thread of our life" but as "one of those threads which are woven into the design of our existence from its beginning to its end."[14] With this "thread," the sign of our finitude, we are called to live, both now and at the "end." "There is a world of difference," writes Dr. Whale, "between 'dying' (a purely zoological fact, admittedly) and 'having to die' (which is uniquely and poignantly human)."[15] And the latter, after all, reminds us of our limitation quite as much as the former.

Limitation, even in its form of death, is not the fundamental reason why we are not immediately fulfilled by deity. Unlike some Oriental religions, Christianity does not maintain that finitude is a mark of evil, or infinitude a sign of good. We do not seek the meaning of our personal existence in being swallowed up in the "infinite," or in being strangely inflated to the dimensions of "infinite selves." If we are to find fulfillment and significance, it must be proportional to our capacities and structure as finite selves. It cannot come by destruction of the self.

Finitude inheres in the nature of personal being. Sin, on the other hand, presupposes finitude by its rebellion against it. Finitude is given with our creation; sin by the act of the total self which conceives creatureliness to be intolerable. Every evidence of limitation in the sight of sin becomes an invitation to do battle against our inferior status as finite beings. Our futile efforts to become as beasts, angels, or gods all have this in common: rebellion against our creatureliness. However, this battle is one which leaves our finitude unshaken but ourselves shaken, guilty, and despairing.

Our attempted defiance of limitation turns out to be a narrowing down to egocentricity of the thoughts and appreciations of the self. The narrower the ground becomes from which we launch our attacks, the more eccentric our attacks become. The narrowing down of our lives, figuratively, comes to a point where stability is problematic. Self-concern turning back upon itself feeds only upon the self, destroying its strength, drawing in the circumference of its appreciations, and producing a kind of dizzy isolation. Thus by turns we reel from self-pity to insolence, from cowardice to rashness, from nameless anxiety to flatulent optimism, from mock docility to obstinate violence, from sentimentality to calculated cruelty, from apathy to frenzied preoccupation with the world. A profound uneasiness and uncertainty seizes us as we find our faculties and actions slipping out of hand on every side. "All things betray thee, who betrayest me," as Francis Thompson said. And the most excruciating pain of all is the frightening loneliness of the self, its inability to reach out to others in sensitive communication and affection. By his inverted interest the sinner locks the door to the maze of his inner life, through whose halls he wanders, disconsolately, yearning for the aid he cannot allow to enter.

Yet sin is not the foolish, wicked deeds we perpetrate on each other. In fact, it is not an ethical category but an ontic one, for it has to do with our fundamental posture toward the whole of related existence. So it cannot be nailed down to any one vice such as pride (though pride is its most frequent and insidious expression), ignorance (though the sinner does not know wherein his true good lies), or sexual lust (though the satisfaction of sexual appetites provides an immediate sense of ecstatic transport which seems to overleap our finitude). Insofar as we can speak in general terms of sin, it appears as a persistent treason or disloyalty to what we at the same time dimly apprehend to be the character of the ground of our existence. It is a disobedience to the claim which the integrity of being makes upon us. It represents a disruption of the fabric of related being which issues in a distortion of perspective, a false image of our position in respect to nature, man, and God. It is an attempt to deny that we are set over against the mystery, power, and love of God. It is estrangement from that which ultimately sustains us, and it turns into a fertile source of concrete evil as we strive to fill up an empty world with a flood of self-interested vanities. At last, sin is the strenuous effort to repudiate the primal faith which constitutes our existence.

Nevertheless, primal faith by its inevitable demand for personal meaning, by its inescapable memory of dependence upon the Other, is the vestigial trace of Him from whose hand we can never free ourselves. As Canon Raven rightly suggests, the feelings of frustration and guilt imply "a criterion which they do not originate or explain."[16] So our efforts at autonomy serve only by their resultant scars of despair, loneliness, and meaninglessness to remind us that there exists One against whom our disloyalty and unfaithfulness are initiated.

To say this much about our human situation is already to pass from the realm of primal faith to that of radical faith. Primal faith discovered may indicate our absolute dependence, but it does not resolve the situation of spiritual and moral ambiguity in which we find ourselves. Nor is the self, rebellious against its creaturehood, in any mood to receive an answer to its question of personal meaning. It cannot hear an answer because in the depth of its own meaninglessness it has already determined that whatever answer it receives must be acceptable to it as it now stands constituted. The answer must be one which leaves the self unchanged, dominant over the answer rather than receptive to it. Yet because sin is a state of being, it can be transformed only by another act of being, an event which has the power to alter the conditions within which the answer will be a true answer to man's need. What is called for is not a new idea so much as a meeting with a reality which puts us "on the spot" of decision. From this point we may look back to interpret what has been happening to us in primal faith, and look ahead with fresh resolution and understanding to the future. "It is futile," Kant said, "to try to become a better man in parts . . . the founding of a character implies the absolute unity of a man's principles and his way of life. . . ."[17] There must be the coincidence of existence and idea, and for that eventuality one must see himself placed decisively before God. The engagement which takes place there is radical faith.

Only from the standpoint of this kind of faith can we begin to see what is involved in existing as beings in faith. Then we see that all along we have lived out of the goodness, justice, mercy, and power of the divine. We could not have denied Him or sought Him unless He had been presupposed by our lives all the time. Unless we already had lived by primal faith, there would have been no quest for meaning, no rebellion against our finitude. But now all this is seen from beyond itself, in our willingness to trust Him as sovereign over all.

In radical faith the Prodigal recognizes that he has never succeeded in breaking his Father's grasp upon him. The substance which was divided to him, now wasted in a far country, and his very existence have been given by the Father. When he comes to himself, he sees his own pitiful estate; he returns to accept a status of unconditional dependence in openness to the forgiving love of the Father. He is welcomed not as a runaway slave but as one who belongs in the Father's house. The "Whither shall I go from thy Spirit?" receives its answer in a returned son, who was dead and is alive again, lost and now found.

II

Some Misunderstandings of Faith

Commit your way to the Lord; trust in him, and he will act.
[Psalm 37:5]

For I would have you know, brethren, that the gospel which
was preached by me is not man's gospel. For I did not receive
it from man, nor was I taught it, but it came through a revelation
of Jesus Christ. [Galatians 1:11-12]

. . . remain at Ephesus that you may charge certain persons
not to teach any different doctrine, nor to occupy themselves with
myths and endless genealogies which promote speculations rather
than the divine training that is in faith; whereas the aim of our
charge is love that issues from a pure heart and a good conscience
and sincere faith. [I Timothy 1:3b-5]

Therefore, my beloved, . . . work out your own salvation with
fear and trembling; for God is at work in you, both to will and
to work for his good pleasure. [Philippians 2:12-13]

PRIMAL faith, as we have suggested, is discoverable; radical faith, on
the other hand, must be consciously enacted. Primal faith is the
mark of a bond with an anonymous ground of existence passively
accepted; radical faith comes in the crisis of fateful decision. Primal
faith, when seen from beyond itself, bespeaks our absolute dependence and finitude; radical faith meets the threat of man's
rebellion against dependence and finitude. Primal faith implies
"something" which "gives" existence and value, from the other
side of finitude; radical faith "crosses over" by venturing to affirm
the existence and character of what stands on the other side and

26

dares, amid the potential meaninglessness of life, to trust what it finds or what is discovered to it. Of this radical faith we will primarily be speaking henceforth.

Radical faith, I propose, is not a possible hypothesis about life's significance, nor is it the postulation of some imaginary being to which to cling through thick and thin. It is, rather, an unreserved act of self-commitment to the Reality which so convincingly makes Himself known to our deepest selves—through Christ, nature, human fellowship, and the struggles of one's own existence—that His existence is indubitable. Such faith is both the continuing engagement of the self with the Determiner of Destiny and the stance of the total self during the engagement. It is not, Walter Lippmann once put it, "a formula which is agreed to if the weight of evidence favors it. It is a posture of man's whole being which predisposes him to assimilate, not merely to believe, his creed."[1] For the Christian, however, what is "assimilated" is not a creed, but the reality which he is convinced keeps struggling with and against him, and to which a creed may point, but which it never completely expresses.

Clearly one is not argued into radical faith.[2] If our subsequent exposition of it is correct, radical faith is above all what each man must come to by himself, and it cannot, therefore, be "proved" in the accepted sense of that word, that is, by empirical evidence or logical coherence. We can but hope to help another come to the "edge" of decision, at which point he and God must "fight it out" together. We can, on the other hand, clarify our view of radical faith by comparison with alternative views of faith which we believe either falsify or give partial interpretations of it. Confession calls for discriminating evaluation as well as exposition.

"I have to have some things I believe with all my heart. That's what faith is, some beliefs you can hold with absolute certainty no matter what happens." In this remark the young student stated man's yearning for the unchanging, the definite, and the final in the midst of much which is changeable, vague, and inconclusive. He could spell out his faith with some precision. He believed that God existed and was omnipotent and all-loving; that Jesus was a great teacher of "spiritual" and ethical ideals which men should follow; that men inclined to be "good" more than "bad," and could by effort develop their "spiritual" and moral life; and that there was some kind of life after death. As he understood it, this was the content of his faith. The form of his faith was the absolute certainty with which he embraced these ideas as true and final.

What a person believes is of crucial import to his life. Any total assessment of his faith must eventually do justice to it. However, we choose here to direct attention not to the *what* but to the *how* of this conception of faith, postponing until Chapter V consideration of *content*. We are asking what form or attitude is involved in the holding of faith according to our student's outlook? How is this conception of the "how" of faith different from that which we find in radical faith?

Marcel has observed that "when a man says that he is convinced, he puts up a sort of barrier. He claims the assurance that nothing which may happen later will modify his way of thinking."[3] He has taken a stand in such a way that he is not "open" to experience or to the mandate of the God in whom he may profess to believe. He "believes *that*" certain ideas are true and valuable; he does not "believe *in*" the reality for which the ideas purport to stand, to follow Marcel's distinction. But faith in a radical sense signifies that my existence is at the disposal of what I trust, that I am not commanding it by the present set of my opinions and judgments. If this is the case with faith, it follows that faith is not an unalloyed certainty but rather a perpetual insecurity before the God who claims my allegiance. Christian faith must then be not a calculated prudence, but in Abbé de Saint-Cyran's phrase "an unequalled and universal flexibility." By it the soul does not grab at certainty but yields to the promptings of Him in whom faith rests.[4]

Consequently, faith incorporates not only assurance and hope but doubt, by virtue of which it is not knowledge. Both doubt and confidence mingle because the self has not encompassed the tension between the majesty and graciousness of God, on one hand, and the finitude and sin of man, on the other.[5] The consummation of the self's destiny has not been achieved; there is something which yet lies in the balance for which a risk must be taken. Faith, as the author of Hebrews puts it, is "the assurance of things *hoped for, the conviction of things not seen.*"[6] A knife-edge, as it were, has to be walked by the finite being who stands before the Eternal. "Trust itself includes a trembling," Aulén has it, "which does not cease during this life, because man is man and God is God."[7] It is this "trembling" or dubiety about one's personal destiny or fulfillment which penetrates lively faith. If God is a living soul, if He does something in human life, that something is not of such a kind that we can neatly confine it in a scheme of beliefs. He marches, and so must the person for whom He has become the Lord of life. Alertness and sensitivity rather than a crouching behind the bulwarks of a "creed" are the orders of the day. Thus Luther could write, "Faith does not require information, knowledge, or security, but a free surrender and joyful daring upon an unfelt, untried, unknown goodness."[8] Here in the deepest sense is doubt and risk, but also that confidence, joy, and assurance which come from a faith into which we fully enter.

But let us return to another aspect of the student's statement about faith. He apparently attached his certainty to the beliefs themselves, thereby creating another confusion. He has identified faith with reports about faith. Propositions, freighted with the intellectual and cultural relativities of the past, have been substituted for the faith relation itself. When this happens, we have commenced the fateful and sometimes disastrous journey from "faith" to "the faith." From trusting God, we begin to pass by easy stages to trusting in statements about Him, or to trusting in those who have formulated and sanctioned these statements. From trusting in Him we slip into trusting the Bible, popes, clergymen, councils, professors, or the Church writ large. From confession of faith we turn to the "confession of the Faith."[9]

This transition took place early in the development of Christianity and continues to this day.[10] Right belief or orthodoxy became a condition of acceptance into the Church and was often substituted for faith in the living God of Jesus Christ. The confidence of Christ in God, and of Paul through Christ in God, gave way to articles of belief about Christ, God, the Holy Spirit, and the Church. The need for a growing movement to stake out its distinctive witness and to distinguish itself from other religious tendencies was obvious. The status of heretic and schismatic must be defined, and the church must have order and discipline. Under persecution and minority status, the central affirmations for which men would suffer and die must be clarified. The creeds, as confessions of faith, became after much conflict and disagreement criteria of membership, rallying points for renewed dedication, and the grounds of certainty concerning salvation itself.

The First Epistle of John shows the tendency: "By this you know the spirit of God; every spirit which confesses that Jesus Christ has come in the flesh is of God, and every spirit which does not confess Jesus is not of God."[11] The Second Epistle carries the same vein: "Anyone who goes ahead and does not abide in the doctrine of Christ does not have God; he who abides in the doctrine of Christ has both the Father and the Son. If anyone comes to you and does not bring this doctrine, do not receive him into the house or give him any greeting, for he who greets him shares his wicked work."[12] In the early church fathers, fighting enemies without and disruptions within the church, the necessity of articulating the faith continued. Irenaeus against the Gnostics, Hippolytus against the Novatians, Origen against Celsus, Tertullian against paganism—these heroically labored to launch the nascent Christian movement but also helped to fasten, as did Nicaea and Chalcedon, the primacy of creed upon the church, until in our own day, in the Roman Church especially, we have the apotheosis of the basic confusion of faith and the faith. So the knowledge of God itself is firmly fixed to the limitations of one branch of the Christian community by the author who writes, "These expressed judgments of faith are enunciated in the form of articles of faith, that is, the propositions of a religious creed. These articles of faith are the first principles of man's knowledge of God."[13] And if we push further with this fateful identification of faith and belief, we discover that faith considered "from the point of view of the truths which are to be believed about God" can yield only "one faith," and that "the Christian faith as expressed in the articles of the Catholic Creed is the one true faith."[14] Various forms of Protestantism have not been far behind in making similar identifications.

Faith necessarily expresses itself in articles of belief. Its confessions not only exhibit the hidden attachments of one's life but also manifest the common convictions of the fellowship in which they arise, for faith is never purely individualistic. However, when professions of faith are transformed into the objects of faith, or where they in turn are used as the basis for pronouncements about one's own or another's spiritual estate, faith in its full sense is no longer speaking. Faith conceived as acceptance of propositions or articles of belief reflects the transition from dependence upon and trust in God to confidence in the fallible and finite products of human ingenuity, no matter how sincerely held. The sovereignty of God is impugned for the benefit of the creature whose works these creeds are. The author of salvation is no longer the object of faith but a product of men. Religion is substituted for faith.[15] When this happens, the essential question becomes "What truths ought I to accept to insure peace, salvation, hope, or certainty?" rather than "In whom or what, that sustains and transforms my being, shall I completely trust?" The difference between faith and belief was unmistakably set forth in the Epistle of James: "You believe that God is one; you do well, even the demons believe—and shudder."[16] The shuddering demon who believes is scarcely the model for Christian faith!

Thus when faith is understood as a search for personal or ecclesiastical certitude, it is betrayed, for it has become, however disguised, a tool by which to secure some value prized for oneself or one's group. It is concerned for a subjective good which can be appropriated rather than the glorification of Him from whom all good comes. The vibrant intercourse with God, codified, degenerates into self-concern and defensiveness. The unheroic soul cowers behind doctrine, hoping against hope that the stroke of God will not destroy what he has carefully erected. The measure of certitude and peace achieved by these tactics robs the soul of its freedom and its birthright of spiritual agony by premature consolation.

Right belief wants rectitude and assurance at all costs. Therefore it circumscribes the area of faith, lest trust go too far. Assent and submission are its characteristic demands, not personal decision. Let all be arranged as quickly as possible for the young or wavering! Save them from the useless buffeting of passion, hope, despair, and lostness, lest they plumb the deeps of their own existence and be found of God Himself. Hold "the faith," and there will be no standpoint beyond it from which it may be questioned. And if radical faith impertinently raises its head, let it be speedily understood how detrimental such free decision is to public morals, good sense, or decent order in church and state. We are counseled to try anything but that desperate "remedy" of faith where each goes out for himself, as indeed he must finally, for the confrontation which shakes him to the roots of his being. Indeed such faith is dangerous! It threatens both belief and the believer, as it lays both open to the unpredictable invasion of God's power and grace. In its hiddenness, faith remains inaccessible to the manipulation of men and their systems, which covet its extraordinary power but refuse its toll.

Popular Protestantism of a liberal tinge and secularism in its less sophisticated expressions also have their distinctive distortions of faith. In repudiating what seems to them the creedalism and attendant legalism of the orthodox, they see themselves emancipated from "dogmatism" and moving toward the freedom of the responsible individual. They are, however, only playing another variation on the same theme of the confusion of faith with belief—the belief in sincerity and intention. Faith in faith is no less an aberration of radical faith than is faith in a set of propositions. In neither case does faith push through to its source and goal. It attempts, rather, to justify itself by calling attention to its earnestness, sincerity, intensity, or reasonableness—all qualities presumably achievable by the person. Nor is there found here an escape from the "dogmatism" which flecks orthodoxies of various types. The dogma of the self's ability to save itself by dint of its zeal and diligence is no less a dogma, even when it cloaks its finite character in the embroideries of apparent candor.

To believe in one's faith, of course, proves a spiritual short circuit. In it I meet myself coming back. The very self wherein lie the deepest discords and confusions does not free itself from them by pronouncing the sincerity of its intentions to do so. Such an assertion becomes instead the projection of a desire for personal integrity rather than the announcement of its realization. If I summon up my energies to trust in my trust, it is I who possess the faith. It is mine, and I, in all my brokenness and partiality, am reflected in this faith, especially when I attempt to control the conditions of its coming. The self-interest and concern which haunts my existence makes impossible the confession "my faith has made me whole." If it is faith of my own contrivance, it can never transform me. The circle of self has been opened at no point.

The peculiar delusion of faith in faith comes from the denial of one's dependence, limitation, and sin. It arises from the presumptions of human sovereignty expressing itself in the view that our salvation is in our own hands. We will not allow that faith has in it anything of the grace of God. It begins and ends with ourselves. Because we dimly sense the need for faith—indeed, because we are inevitably drawn to trust—we may attempt to draw up from the bottomless reservoir of the self those feelings and attitudes we assume properly belong to religion.

The answer to this fruitless effort Luther put clearly enough:

Faith is not the human fancy and dream which some people mistake for faith. When such persons see that no amendment of the life and no good works follow, although they may hear and talk much about faith, they fall into error and declare that faith is not enough, but we must perform good works if we would be pious and attain salvation. In consequence of this, when they hear the Gospel, they fail to work and frame for themselves by their own powers a notion in their hearts which says, I believe. This they then consider true faith. But as it is a human invention and notion, of which the heart in its depth finds out nothing, it accomplishes also nothing and no amendment of the life follows. But faith is a divine work in us, which transforms us and begets us anew from God. . . .[17]

Whatever else we may call the dredging operations in the soul, they do not constitute radical faith. Concentrations upon the inner feeling of the self may conjure up the sentiment of faithfulness, but it remains at last one more mark of our separation from the source of our existence.[18]

Perhaps the most widespread view of faith connects it with the problem of how we know in any field, but especially in matters religious. In this respect, Aquinas gave faith one of its classical formulations when he recognized it as "essentially cognitive" and thus belonging properly to the intellect.[19] The faith which seeks to apprehend divine or supernatural truth is "a habit of mind, whereby eternal life is begun in us, making the intellect assent to what is non-apparent."[20] The prevailing mood of Thomas's theology is that of the Greek mind, which assumes the goal of life to be knowledge —in Thomas's case the knowledge of God or the Beatific Vision. Reason or active intellect is one essential identifying character of mankind and must be perfected at last in the knowledge of God. Because such knowledge is normally hidden from man in this life, as we deal only with the effects of God's action, the perfection of both the will and the intellect awaits the life after death. In the meantime, however, man must believe certain truths about God, Christ, the Holy Spirit, the Church, etc., which, although not contrary to reason, are above its ability to seize directly. Men need divine truth now and cannot await the development of their intellectual capacity to make clear this truth. Therefore, "in order that men might have knowledge of God, free of doubt and uncertainty, it was necessary for divine truths to be delivered to them by way of faith, being told to them, as it were, by God Himself who cannot lie."[21] Thus faith came to be considered both as the means by which divine truth is imparted and as the body of truths, themselves sanctified by the Church. These two falsifications of faith

Aquinas helped to fasten securely on Christianity.

Faith, by his reading, seemed fated to become a short cut to salvation for those who lacked the aptitude and patience to become saints or doctors of divinity. It was a capsule prepared by wise and holy men, certified as being rational and necessary by a powerful institution. Indeed, it could be counted a speedy medicine for human spiritual and moral ills. Unfortunately for such a view of faith, man finds it does not square with his own experience. He must still come to personal decisions for himself at some point before the face of God Himself. No church, no wise theologian or creed can serve as substitute for one's own encounter with deity—a fact which Thomas in his mysticism verified before his death.

It cannot be denied that Thomas offered a persuasive and skillful handling of the problem of faith and reason. However, his inclusion of faith within the realm of cognition or knowledge presents difficulties which we should at least mention in passing. In the first place, he assumed, as do many who follow him, that faith is a noetic relation, that is, that faith is a way of knowing God. A more careful analysis of the nature of faith might have revealed to him what Buber in our own day has pointed out. This noted Jewish scholar holds that "philosophy understands faith as an affirmation of truth lying somewhere between clear knowledge and confused opinion." Religion, on the other hand, insofar as it speaks of knowledge at all, he continues, "does not understand it as a noetic relation, but rather as mutual contact, as the genuinely reciprocal meeting . . . between one active existence and another."[22] It is unlikely that Thomas could have acquiesced in this conclusion, as he assumed, in the second place, that deity enjoyed perfection.

This perfection is conceived primarily by Aquinas in the philosophical tradition of Aristotle, rather than that of the predominant Biblical testimony. Perfection signified for him absence of potentiality in the divine being. There is nothing that rightfully pertains to divine existence which He might become or choose, or by which He can be changed. There is no deficiency in deity; hence there is no imperfection or changeability in Him. "God" as a modern commentator on Aquinas points out, "does not persist through change; God is changeless."[23] This conception of God obviously makes of deity a static rather than a dynamic being. It is scarcely necessary to suggest that Thomas attempted to relate this view of divine perfection to the Biblical outlook. That he succeeded in working out the synthesis between Biblical categories and Aristotelian meta-physics may be fairly questioned, impressive as was his effort.

Operating within the limits of his conception of perfection, Thomas finds it difficult to envisage the "meeting" of "one active existence and another." Such a deity would be presumed to be an object to be known by analogy, inference from effects, or mystical insight, but not one who actively strove with men in the thick of their own existence. As a being to be known, He is indifferent to being known, as is any inanimate object of human knowledge. Thus by combining the conception of static perfection with a formulation of the God-man relation along noetic lines, Thomas misinterpreted the religious situation.

Another difficulty presented by the Thomistic position brings together his view of revelation and his confidence in human reason. Thomas conceded the finitude of human reason and correspondingly made place for revelation and the supernatural in his system. However, according to his rationalistic hypothesis, he conceived revelation to consist of a series of religious truths or propositions offered to the reason supernaturally. Such doctrines as Creation and the Trinity are therefore conceived as above or beyond unaided reason, but not contrary to it. The reason may not initially conclude to these truths, but once they are opened to it, it may attest their truth by the tests of rational discourse. Again, what is assumed is that revelation consists of the disclosure of "knowledge" about God rather than "knowledge" of a meeting with God. "It is information received by the mind rather than existence transformed."[24] Furthermore, it is assumed that reason is completely impervious to the encroachments of sin. It is therefore capable, apart from revelation or faith in any transformative sense, of knowing the truth about God. Both of these assumptions, it will be seen, are open to serious question.

This characteristic misreading of faith in the Thomistic view may be further clarified by pointing up the crucial difference between "thinking" the truth in the form of propositions, and "being" in the truth. The truth for Thomas is that which is held by the intellect or accepted by the will in an act of belief, i.e., faith. However, for a deeper reading of truth one must see it as a disposition or bent of the total self by which it is disposed to enact or assimilate truthfulness. Prior to "knowing" the "truths" of science, theology, or any other field, there must be a readiness to "see," the sensitivity and fidelity to what is given to one in experience. Thus truth may be regarded as an event, or process, rather than an operation of one segment of the self, e.g., the reason or the will.

For Christianity, Tillich tells us, truth is not a series of propositions discovered or found, as it is for the Greek frame of mind. "Truth is something new, something which is *done* by God in history, and because of this, something which is *done* in the individual life. . . . The mystery of truth in Christianity is an event which has taken place and which takes place again and again. . . . In Greek thought truth only can be found. In Christianity truth is found if it is done, and done if it is found."[25] Of this existential reading of truth the Thomistic position has little to say. Faith remains for it in the cognitive realm, and truth consists of propositions and articles of belief.

Some liberal Protestant thinkers move along similar lines while repudiating the creedalism of Roman Catholicism. We are informed, for example, that faith is a rational supposition based upon past experience projected toward future possibilities. It is the thrusting forward of a reasonable person's views, tentatively held, awaiting the confirmation or denial of relevant evidence. One contemporary author defines faith as the "conscious willingness to move along and develop one stream of activity on the basis of incomplete evidence because it is, nevertheless, the most reasonable course possible in that situation." Or stated more concisely, "Faith is the willingness to act in accordance with the most reasonable hypothesis."[26]

In spite of the emphasis upon action in this definition, it conceives faith primarily as intellective and theoretical.[27] Faith is here treated as the entertainment of a theory about life without the engagement of the self in that theory. The crucial question of the self which holds in check the other streams of activity while one stream is developed is left quite untouched. By what is this self living? Upon what does it depend? From what does it derive strength and insight in the meantime? Can I calmly and rationally move ahead to verify a hypothesis about God's goodness, immortality, etc., quite unaffected in the interim by the consequences of my experiment? Who indeed is this disposer of hypotheses about destiny who acts only "because" a certain theory is most rational? Where do I find this "person" within me? I do not, as it were, discover him involved in the hypotheses themselves, for he is the proposer and judge of the hypotheses. The self which does the proposing and verifying seems to live at a quite different level from that referred to by the proposed theory.

This means that as I am not genuinely involved in the hypothesis at the outset, neither am I profoundly involved in its outcome. If this particular theory does not work to my satisfaction, if it breaks my conception of what is rationally to be expected, if it appears to demand a conversion of my spiritual estate, I am free to try another "research experiment" until I get one which does suit me.

But what if this trial be conceived in broader dimensions? What if the experiment be one I must make with my whole life? What if there is no second chance to verify results, because there really is no more time for my life? The whole of my life must be in the hypothesis in its total duration. So Dorothy Emmet reminds us, "Testing something at the risk of one's life is not quite the same as testing something with the whole of one's life." We may come, under these circumstances, to change our standards of success, that is, be changed in depth and at last hold to God "in spite of apparent disaster by all human standards, including our own."[28] Gone then is the semidetached observer, for the self is in fact in the experiment. The conditions of scientific hypothesis are irrelevant. Predictability and the notion of "all things being equal," so necessary for the scientific method, are shattered. Courage, not prudence, is called for, and the element of "in spite of" evidence comes into play.

Some "hypotheses" of radical Christian faith, if such they can be called, cut much deeper into human existence than the definition proposed. They have to do with death and life, sin and guilt, estrangement and reconciliation, despair and hope, God's judgment and mercy, and for these no piecemeal approach suffices. They are the kinds of experiences which promise irretrievable disaster or substantial success. They place the self in jeopardy and question and deny the power of the self to question them and decide them validly on its own grounds. They speak to man, in his trembling and awe, of a Reality which already "knows" us before we "know" Him. The tables are turned. We are the tried in the hypothesis, not the experimenters. We are not at the center of the stage, pushing out venturesome guesses toward the dubious "out there." We discover ourselves as under a scrutiny which goes to the heart of our existence.[29]

Thomism and the type of liberal Protestantism sketched above share the view that faith is a temporary step on the way to the rational apprehension of truth or the vision of God. This outlook apparently stems in the first instance from the failure to distinguish between primal faith and radical faith, and the distinctive roles each plays in human existence. Primal faith, it will be recalled, is the inescapable witness to our finitude and absolute dependence. As such it is not an optional factor in human life, to be eliminated by growth in knowledge. It remains the presupposition of human existence, and therefore of all knowledge, regardless of how it is attained. Radical faith is a continuing, conscious decision made by the self as a whole as it confronts the power, grace, and mystery of God. It is an act of existence, not of reason operating in isolation. Radical faith stands face to face with infidelity, meaninglessness, pride, and, in short, sin. It is not part of the continuum which runs from ignorance, through opinion and belief, to full knowledge. It is one of the conditions of rational knowledge, but it cannot be analyzed without remainder as a provisional, and finally expendable, adjunct in reason's search for truth. It keeps step with existence in a way which beliefs do not, for we exchange the latter for more adequate conceptions as we experience and think our way toward what we take to be truth. Radical faith is in large part the consciously adopted posture toward the meaning of existence as a whole; so long as one's life lasts, this continuing wrestle with the mystery of existence and the sin of which we become aware goes on. It cannot be cast aside by an increase of knowledge, because the mystery which evokes it does not simply lie ahead of us as a problem to be solved in the future. Mystery inheres in the here and now of our existence and in whatever knowledge we achieve. It does not vanish at the touch of reason's clear light, for there remains at least the mystery of the rational process itself.

In the second place, radical faith cannot be dispensed with in this world by reason because sinlessness seems to lie beyond our capabilities. Increase in rational apprehension does not overcome sin, because the reason is itself embedded in the life of the sinner. As such it does not transcend or conquer sin as we have conceived it above. Brunner has put it this way: "The more . . . we are concerned with the 'personal heart' of human existence, the less sure is reason, the more limited is the autonomy which can be ascribed to it, the more sinister becomes its self-sufficient attitude and its claim to recognition."[30] In view of the vigor of Brunner's words, it is perhaps well to point out that I am not subscribing either to the view that reason is hopelessly corrupt, incapable of coming to any truth about the self, or to the view that reason as such "sins." Man is the sinner, not some function of man. Yet it may be pointed out that reason is affected by the context of personal existence in which it resides. It does not, as it comes to the ultimate questions, move with the clarity and surety which it shows in dealing with physics or astronomy. By itself it cannot overcome sin because it is self-concerned even when it is aware that it is self-concerned! Therefore, the notion that increase of knowledge automatically takes one beyond the need of faith as the answer to sin is open to question. We cannot repudiate reason, but neither can we put sole dependence upon it within the framework of human limitation and sin. We should falsify the status of neither reason nor faith.

Reason itself points beyond its own limits to the nature of being in which it participates. We could not operate as human beings unless we accepted quite absolutely the idea that the "logos" of man has the deepest relations to the "logos" of the universe. The threadbare argument that reason cannot be denied without the use of reason and a complete confidence in its capacities is scarcely the triumph for pure reason which its proponents imagine. Whoever in his right mind ever denied this dialectical cul-de-sac? But what are the implications of this circular argument? What faith sees here is not a demonstration of the autonomy and self-sufficiency of reason but an evidence of the coercive structure of reality which makes the argument valid. Reason does not *determine* reality; reality determines the course which reason must follow to secure a true answer. Reason points to the form of existence which makes its own pronouncements valid or invalid. Radical faith, therefore, does not deny the place of reason in its confession; it sees it rather as one more indication of the divine gift to man, which, when informed by faith, directs the mind back to the giver. While faith does not demand the sacrifice of intellect, it refuses to be treated as a mere auxiliary to it, as though reason were an autonomous function of the self, never spotted by sin, reigning supreme over a lower realm of will and emotion.[31] Faith challenges reason to be more, not less, critical of its presuppositions, to take seriously its limits and liability to self-concern, and to penetrate as deeply as possible into the matrix of the divine-human encounter. Faith calls reason to recognize, in a responsible manner, its participation in human existence at its fullest when it is lived under the sovereignty not of itself but of God.[32]

My concluding clarification deals with two phrases which may give difficulty in respect to the distinction between primal and radical faith. These phrases are "Christian faith" and "the Christian faith." Clearly, the two phrases are closely related, but they are not identical in significance. And so far neither has been identified with primal or radical faith—though it is evident that the latter term has already established contact with Christian faith in my thought. Primal faith has been regarded as the inevitable mode of existence for finite man as an unconditionally dependent being, face to face with the mystery of his own existence. But it has also been made clear that a reflexive act of some kind, a shock or accident is necessary if man is to be aware of this subtle "acceptance" of existence. It must be seen, as it were, from beyond itself to be recognized and interpreted as part of the fuller meaning of human existence. Radical faith, in one aspect, provides the viewpoint or perspective from which such identification and interpretation takes place. It is the radical turning of the whole being of man to what he conceives to be of ultimate and absolute significance and reality, given his own finitude and sin. But radical faith is also the opening of the ultimate mystery to man. It is an engagement of what is transhuman with the human; it is an encounter of man with God, and God with man. It is then also a gift, not only an achievement of desperate human beings. It is the point where for the person in faith the mystery becomes luminous; where something "breaks through" in such convincing and converting power that a new foundation is laid for his existence henceforth. Although its pronouncements may not be greeted with universal acceptance by those who have not felt the power of such an encounter, it remains the absolute center and source for the individual's life. It provides the framework or perspective for interpreting and validating all subsidiary assumptions. It provides the strength out of which to live and die.[33]

For the Christian the crucial point at which the mystery has become luminous is Jesus Christ, or more accurately, the God who is revealed through Jesus Christ. What Jesus Christ did and taught becomes the clue to understanding both ourselves and deity. He is the concrete and absolute manifestation of the divine, and therefore, for the Christian, radical faith focuses upon him. Radical faith is Christian faith when in humility we find the opening into the mystery of our existence through Christ. Christian faith takes seriously Christ as the revelatory event in one's personal history, but it does so knowing that this opportunity, so far as modern man is concerned, comes through a community and a Bible. The meeting with God through Christ is not a purely atomistic act by a single self and God; but neither is it a mass phenomenon, an automatically reproducible experience on a grand scale. Christian faith is of the individual, but by its very nature it is not simply for the individual. It links hands, by deeds, words, and symbols, with the whole community across the centuries which have found in this man, Jesus Christ, the transformative power over human sin. By its insights, its fellowship, and service the community nourishes the life in faith; and the life in faith in turn nurtures the life of the community. But both the community and the individual stand under the claim of the God of Jesus Christ. Neither can absolutize itself before Him. The community cannot cynically identify its pronouncements with the divine word; nor can the individual run off into arbitrary and eccentric isolation. Both stand in continuing dialogue with each other under the sovereign rule of God. The will of God, Christian faith proclaims, stands over and beyond our garbled and fragmentary utterances, even when these have been written down by our spiritual forebears in the Bible. Out of this continuing dialogue between community, self, and God there emerge the creeds, dogmas, platforms, and confessions of the church. But these also are the by-products of faith, not its norms and sanctions.

The phrase "the Christian faith" takes its proper place in this context of a living community under the God of Jesus Christ. Systems of belief, creeds, the structures of thought framed by theologians, the "vocabulary," symbols, traditions, and ritual constitute "the Christian faith." These elements furnish the visible and specific means of communication between generations of Christians. They insure continuity of conviction and forestall aberrations of thought and interpretation. They serve as rallying points for re-dedication and renewal, enlightenment and education. They are the slowly moving framework of interpretation for faith's venture and are responsive, even if but tardily, to fresh discoveries of radical faith. But Christian faith can never be identified with "the Christian faith." The life in faith, Christian faith, is the substance of which "the Christian faith" is the formalized, rationalized, and conservative structure. "Christian faith" refers to the church within and beyond the church; "the Christian faith" refers to the institutionalized, historically conditioned church in its more static forms—though even "the Christian faith" never stands still. P. T. Forsyth had the right of the matter when he asserted, "I am not saved by the apostle or his experience, nor by the Church and its experience, but by what saved the apostle and the Church."[34]

It is easy to rail at dogma and tradition, the structure of the church and liturgy, as though they were unmitigated evils set in the path of faith. It is equally easy to become defensive about these functions of the church, as though the Ark of the Lord would fall if we did not put forth our hands to steady it. Yet faith stands not in opposition to these structures of belief and practice, except as they usurp the place of the Lord of the church. It finds them rather as the pole with which it must continue to stand in tension, lest it be turned into sheer arbitrariness, and the church into a monolithic and unyielding structure. Each represents a moment in the total life of the Christian which may be likened, somewhat lamely, to the progress of a stream. Dogma and doctrine are like the banks of the stream of vital faith. They are formed by the deposits of the stream itself, yet as banks they guide and direct the stream, even while undergoing erosion. The banks are not inert masses of rock, but rich earth which repeatedly is caught up in the flow of the stream and is redistributed. The power of radical faith prevents the clogging of the stream; the temporary rigidity of the banks gives direction and unity to the stream. It was Archbishop Temple who wrote, "Faith is not the holding of correct doctrines, but personal fellowship with the living God. Correct doctrines will both express this, and assist it and issue from it; incorrect doctrine will misrepresent this and hinder and prevent this. . . . I do not believe in any creed, but I use certain creeds to express, to conserve and to deepen my belief in God."[35] And with this conclusion radical faith has no quarrel.

III

Faith and Christ

And Jesus said to him, "Why do you call me good? No one is good but God alone." [Mark 10:18]

Blessed are the pure in heart, for they shall see God. [Matthew 5:8]

And Jesus cried out and said, "He who believes in me, believes not in me but in him who sent me. And he who sees me sees him who sent me." [John 12:44-45]

Father, if thou art willing, remove this cup from me; nevertheless not my will, but thine, be done. [Luke 22:42]

But God shows his love for us in that while we were yet sinners, Christ died for us. [Romans 5:8]

All this is from God, who through Christ reconciled us to himself and gave us the ministry of reconciliation; that is, in Christ God was reconciling the world to himself. . . . [II Corinthians 5:18-19a]

FOR Christian faith, Jesus Christ is unique. He is the irreplaceable locus of God's revelation. The total event of Christ—his character, life, teachings, death, and resurrection—gives an ineradicable form to the divine revelation, tethering faith to a definite, concrete, historical figure. He possesses, to use the late Donald Baillie's words, "absolute significance" as the point of vantage from which faith understands itself and its engagement with God.[1] The absolute has acted in this inimitable figure to lay open the meaning and purpose of human existence. He constitutes, therefore, the turning

point in history and affords for faith the perspective from which
history itself is to be understood. He lays open the possibility for
a new form of existence for persons, by showing forth God's power,
mercy, and love in a distinctive fashion. He is the norm for that
new form of existence. Yet he points beyond himself to One who
transcends his limits as a finite participant in history, who is not
exhausted in the words and deeds of this one man.

Our information about Jesus is disappointingly meager. Careful
study produces not a biography of a man but the fragments of a
portrait which bear unmistakable marks of originality and authenticity. Much of what he said and did has been lost, or transformed
in the process of oral and written transmission. Probably not all
of his deeds and words were at the time counted of sufficient importance to be remembered or set down. There were periods of
solitude for which now only informed conjecture can account. He
was in the public eye for not more than three years at the most,
and much of that time was passed in insignificant villages on the
outskirts of the Roman Empire. No writing of his has been passed
down to us; no picture of him is available. However, if scientific
biography is out of the question, there nevertheless remains an
outline of his career, a well-substantiated core of his teaching, and
the overtones of a decisive impact upon human beings.

The principal sources for learning of the historical Jesus are the
four gospels, each of which commences with a distinctive introduction. No one story of his origins seemed to have won universal
acceptance, according to what we find in these gospels and in Paul's
letters.[2] Mark, in fact, omits any reference to his birth and begins
with Jesus' baptism by John the Baptizer. At this point all four of
the gospels come together on a common historical basis.[3] Thence-
forth the gospels of Matthew and Luke depend largely upon the
Marcan order of events in Jesus' life, whereas the gospel of John
proceeds with a variant sequence.

Jesus is baptized by John the Baptist in a baptism "of repentance
for the forgiveness of sins."[4] At this time a profound consciousness
of God's call comes upon him, followed by a period of "temptation."
After John's arrest, Jesus begins a preaching and healing mission
in Galilee with the words, "the time is fulfilled, and the Kingdom is
at hand; repent, and believe in the good news [gospel]."[5] During
a period of relative popularity, he chooses twelve disciples from a
larger following. Several sharp interchanges with Pharisees and

scribes take place on points of his authority and Sabbath observance, but in an almost informal way Jesus continues to drive home his points with wit, irony, parable, and dialectical skill. He offends the Pharisees but incites the confidence and hopes of common people. In the district of Caesarea Philippi, Peter owns Jesus as the Christ, and shortly thereafter the fateful journey to Jerusalem begins. In Jerusalem he wins the hatred of the Sadducean party and high priests. He is seized, and after a perfunctory hearing before the council, is turned over to the Roman procurator, Pontius Pilate. As a dangerous troublemaker or rebel against constituted authority he is crucified. His body is buried by a comparative stranger, the disciples having taken cover. The Resurrection appearances occur, but at first only to those who have been his closest followers.[6]

It would be strange if such a skeletal account as this, granted its essential accuracy, should be thought worthy of preservation as a convincing demonstration of Christ's greatness. As one modern writer says, "There was, and still there is, no finally compelling reason enshrined in the bare facts for accepting the Christian affirmations about them."[7] It would be even more surprising if this account as it stands should be taken for a peculiarly distinctive operation of God. From such sorry evidence we could scarcely make intelligible the origin of the Christian movement itself. There must have been more to it—and there was. And this more took place in and through the historical events of Jesus' life and teaching. It is not an embroidery of fancy draped over a stark historical framework; it is bound up with the man Jesus himself. In the events of Jesus' entire career, faith discovers God acting, revealing Himself to men not in abstract principles or truths but in the transformation of personal existence from sin to faith, from death to life. If, as Donald Baillie inquired, we cannot validly find any revelation of God in the portrait of Jesus as a historical person, "how are we ever to reach and accept the dogmas about Him?"[8]

Because the Biblical writers of both the Old and the New Testaments are themselves participants in events by which they have been transformed, they speak as those in faith to others on the way to faith. They are not mere chroniclers of events about which they have no passion or interest. For them history has been and still is being illuminated by great deeds of God which are discernible in specific, yet apparently quite common, experiences. History itself is the arena of divine action—though God is not identified with history. This is His world. He works in it, creating, sustaining, judging, and reconciling it. He is not confined to some distant realm of the "spiritual," nor is He limited only to revealing Himself in the pleasant, peaceful, and beautiful. He is at work in the agony, ugliness, and upheavals of human life. Amid the rise and fall of empires, the overthrow of righteous and unrighteous rulers, treacherous murders and repulsive lechery, family devotion and separations, the sly shifting of boundary markers, the giving of short weight in the market place, the selling of the poor for a pair of sandals, where prophets ecstatically proclaim divine judgment or plaintively woo an erring people to its covenant responsibility, where promises are made of an exuberant day of peace and joy to come—in all these God is pressing in upon mankind for justice, peace, reconciliation, adapting His strategy to meet the free yet often tragic choices of men. He is there in the ambiguities of human designs and actions. But He is not overcome by them. By His power and mercy He is sustaining even the refractory and wicked, while His justice is seen in the downfall of the evildoer and His vindication of the innocent. His compassion is ever extended to the penitent and sorrowing. In the still small voice and the lionlike roar He makes Himself heard above the hurly-burly of humanity's turmoiled existence. He is Lord over His world, but He is not an absentee master.

The New Testament authors never doubt that God's action is discernible in history, but they are confident that they have a new clue to what He is doing with its tangled web. The promises and acts of the old dispensation have now been put in a fresh light by His new act in Christ. The life, the teaching, but pre-eminently the crucifixion and resurrection of this Jesus are the concrete events in which the divine will is made manifest. With a bewildering array of symbols and often inconsistent notions, these writers rush on to proclaim what Christ means to them and can mean to all men. Not for a moment do they pretend to offer a dispassionate account of what has happened. They are not neatly sorting evidence or weighing sources; they write to confess, persuade, and explain. They bring together stories and teachings from the common store of the early church's memory and experience, and pour them out in a rough unity which converges on Christ himself.

He who occupies the center of their message is not an itinerant rabbi, a rustic carpenter bent on a harebrained scheme to overthrow Roman law and Jewish worship, or a dreamy idealist building

castles in the air. No one term will catch up the novelty and power
of this Jesus, so a number of names are used. He is the Christ, the
Messiah, the Anointed One set apart by God. He is Lord and Master, Son of God and Man. He is the Logos, the Word of God. He
is the risen and glorified One, the Lamb of God, the great High
Priest who is himself the sacrifice. "As far back as we can go,"
Forsyth pointed out, "we find only the belief and worship of a
risen, redeeming, and glorified Christ, whom they could wholly
trust, but only very poorly imitate; and in his relation to God could
not imitate at all."[9] In this Christ, they claim, God has expressed
His love and judgment, opening to them a way out of that bondage
to sin and death they know so well. Even as their plight is clarified
to them by his coming, a new hope for reconciliation with God
grows, nourished by the immediate living presence of him who has
loved and will love them to the end of the age.

History assumes a new structure and meaning. No longer is it
the repetition of cycles of weary time, endlessly circling back upon
themselves. No longer is it the patient waiting for the "new age"
of Jewish piety, so long deferred. A decisive event has occurred,
which has straightened out the cycles and fulfilled the hopes for
a new age. Jesus Christ has come, bearing the load of obedient love
for the Father; hence, the new age has been inaugurated. Even
now he continues to live among us; hence the new age is a present
reality. He has risen and will return in indescribable glory; hence
the full consummation of the new age is future. History moves,
for these Christians, under the sway of a continuing judgment
and mercy toward a final judgment and reconciliation. It is not
a helter-skelter of unrelated happenings but a unified drama of salvation.

Certain of the accidental features of this drama, as portrayed in
the New Testament, must be cast aside by a modern Christian, but
the central theme of the drama rings true to the deepest experiences
of man. Christ remains for present-day faith the revelation of God.
He is in fact a double revealer, for at one and the same time he
shows man to himself in his need while revealing God as the ultimate object of his trust. He answers the question "What is man
before the righteous, majestic, yet loving God?" by also answering
the query "What is God before finite, sinful, yet hopefully striving
man?"[10] He is "transparent," to employ Tillich's term, without
subscribing fully to his usage. Through Christ God shows us to

ourselves and at the same moment reveals His love.[11]

How may we construe this double transparency? Take, for example, the Sermon on the Mount as one way of Christ's revealing us to ourselves. When we seriously study the Sermon, we soon realize that its pronouncements and promises are not simple ethical exhortation. They cannot be hung on the walls of our homes as mottoes which urge us daily to try a little harder to be decent. Neither are they blueprints for utopia on earth. They are not a strategy for personal peace or social survival. They do not allay anxiey; rather they provoke despair by reminding us how impossible they are of fulfillment. They upset; they do not comfort. With Mark Twain we have to say, "It is not the parts of the Bible I don't understand that bother me. It's the parts I do understand!"

We can attempt to veer off from Jesus' words by treating them as figures of speech. "Certainly Jesus did not mean I should love my enemies! What did he *really* mean?" Obviously, he could not have commanded anything so contrary to our present inclination or present powers to achieve! But as Knox says, "We try to deceive ourselves into thinking that we owe no more than we can pay."[12] Or we can fall back on the comforting thought that Jesus' teachings are too impractical for life as we know it. We may pay them the dubious honor of calling them "ideals" which guide from afar.

Of course the difficulty lies in the fact that we know we are not judging Christ and his words, but that we are being judged by them both. Christ in his power, speaking through these words, confronts us with a demand which we simply cannot fulfill. He exposes us to our reluctant gaze as those for whom every moral and spiritual confidence is shaken. Complacency and condescension collapse before the simplest line of the Sermon. "The things Jesus says to us in the Sermon on the Mount," Bernhard Anderson writes, "make God's demand so absolute, so inward, so immeasurable, and in the last analysis, so unattainable that no Christian who is honest can parade his righteousness before God and look condescendingly upon the other man as a sinner."[13]

I find I cannot obey, at the crucial point, at the level of my deepest motives and attitudes. How shall "I" command the lust or hate which wells up within, when "I" like to lust or hate? I may be able to refrain from overt adultery and murder, but the imaginations of the heart are quite a different matter. As we read the words of the Sermon, we begin to see that our secret world of sensuality is no longer private. There is One who knows and judges what goes on in there! Squirm as we may from the light of that exposure, it indicts us ruthlessly and absolutely, not by comparison with other men, but with the purity and love of Christ. We may feverishly attempt to recapture our respectability, but strangely enough, we also acquiesce in the justice of the condemnation. Our growing despair arises not simply from our mixed and impure motives but from having to live with them, recognizing their baseness yet incapable of bringing them to heel by some resolute act of will.

There runs through our lives a disquieting duplicity of mind. We see the claim Christ lays upon us as one which can be fulfilled only by single-minded trust in the Father. But we also cast about to secure the promises of Christ as though our devotion should offer us some ulterior reward. And, most distressing of all, we live recognizing that we are drawn in both directions at the same time.

The words "Blessed are the poor in spirit" remind us that we seldom consider ourselves poor in spirit unless we also hope for the solace of the Kingdom. We cannot bear to mourn without the anxious sidelong glance toward the promised comfort. Our meekness, tainted by the will to power, tends to become a means of our inheriting the earth. Our hunger and thirst after righteousness slips into the desire for satisfaction. Our mercy looks hopefully to its repayment. Our purity of heart doubles back on itself as a search for the heavenly vision, and our peacemaking becomes a fierce desire for the supreme title "sons of God." We may be enjoined to seek first the Kingdom and its righteousness, but the search is prompted by the furtive hope that "these things" shall be added unto us. If we are bade to love the Lord our God with all our being, and our neighbors as ourselves, we are pressed to the wall. Who single-mindedly wants to love God, except for the comfort, the strength and blessedness it may bring him? Prudential self-concern has simply brought us to the limit of spiritual exhaustion and despair.

However, the agony which seizes us at this extremity is met by the words of Christ which form the basis of the whole Sermon: "Repent and believe the good news." The teachings of the Sermon are supportable only for those who having truly come to their limit refuse further assault upon it in their own power, and turn in their whole being to Him who has been their accuser. Repentance is the response to the shattering of spiritual and moral complacency:

casting oneself in total trust upon Him who has revealed us to ourselves.

Jesus' words on repentance in the Sermon and elsewhere, the whole impact of his ministry and death bespeak the centrality of repentance for Christian faith. The doorway to radical Christian faith is none other than the complete turning of our being away from its supposed grounding in itself, society, or nature, and the relaxed, grateful acceptance of our being from God's hand, even that disheveled, disunited being we have found ourselves to be.[14] We have been revealed to ourselves not only as judged but as called to conversion, in its legitimate sense. We are the kind of beings who must live in repentance, if we are to live at all before a righteous and gracious deity. Our striving to fulfill the demands of Christ out of unworthy motives must be transformed by our decision to commit ourselves to God. The commitment, indeed, is the beginning of the ordering and purifying of our motives as a whole, since no piecemeal "training" of them is possible. To those who dare to accept the invitation to repentance, a new foundation of personal existence is laid in humility and thankfulness, and words which hitherto signified judgment become descriptions of the new life with Christ. They bespeak mercy and hope because we are placed by faith to hear them as such.

Is this "good news"? If Christ's announcement of the Kingdom means judgment, which it clearly does to the best of us; if repentance is the condition of entry into it, conceived as a promise and hope of fulfillment, in what sense is Christ's coming "good news"? The truth of the matter seems to be that the coming of the Kingdom and Christ is not good news except to those who have come to see their plight and repent. He came "to those who are sick, not to call the righteous, but sinners."[15] To those who are sure of themselves, whose righteousness has never undergone the searching judgment of God, Christ and the Kingdom offer no good news, only persistent judgment. But to those who are surfeited by themselves and their fumbling, repeated attempts at "goodness" by pulling at their own bootstraps, to those who see the shabbiness of their virtue or who have been counted out of the human court of decency and respectable morality, Christ brings "good news." He provides not an intolerable denunciation but an invitation to renewal through God's love and mercy.

To discover God striding toward you through the wreckage of

your self-centered ambitions, to be found of Him in the midst of your flimsily wrought life, and to receive word of Him when the whole business has turned flat and insipid—is not this hope and good news? To awaken to the fact that quietly, in the network of your most earnest and honest desires, Another has been and still is at work to bring them to a meaningful climax, to learn that when you trustfully obey, new passion, fresh verve, and clearer insight appear unbidden, and that when you put your full weight down upon Him, you find yourself sustained through thick and thin—is not this hope and good news? To discover yourself upon the road to freedom from the cloying enticements of the self, from the agonizing battle with moral and religious legalism which you mistook for His service—is there not hope and good news here? To discern at last that you are already thoroughly known by Him, so that the burden of further concealment may be thrown aside—is not this good news? To find your febrile efforts at self-discipline relaxed in a new orientation to Him who stands beyond you—is not this a message of good news and renewed hope? The Kingdom then is not a set of commands. It expresses the kinds of ends which a changed will can accept and for which it aims—not that we achieve, but knowing our God to be merciful and One who seeks above all our trust, we may leave the outcome to Him.

When Calvin discoursed on freedom from the law, he expressed some measure of the good news which is in Christ and the Kingdom. He put it this way:

They who are bound by the yoke of the law, are like slaves who have certain daily tasks appointed by their masters. They think they have done nothing, and presume not to enter into the presence of their masters without having finished the work prescribed to them. But children, who are treated by their parents in a more liberal manner, hesitate not to present to them their imperfect, and in some respects faulty works, in confidence that their obedience and promptitude of mind will be accepted by them, though they have not performed all that they wished. Such children ought one to be. . . .[16]

Thus for faith Christ reveals us to ourselves by the judgment and hope he brings. He does this not by asking us to compare our virtues and vices with each other. He does not even summon us to compare ourselves with himself, as though he represented the ideal or perfect man.[17] He shows us our condition and grounds for assurance by setting us uncompromisingly before the righteousness of

God Himself. "Not everyone who says to me 'Lord, Lord' shall enter the kingdom of heaven, but he who does the will of my Father who is in heaven."[18] In the light of the divine claim, men know that their righteousness must be that of grateful, repentant, obedient service, or willingness to be from moment to moment at His disposal. The revelation of ourselves to ourselves is then carried out by Christ because God reveals Himself in Christ. The two revelations are two sides of one coin. By being transparent to God, Christ makes possible the transparency of the human situation.

The gospels make abundantly clear that Jesus Christ is not God.[19] Yet they are at one in finding in him the triumphant culmination of the acts of God's disclosure set forth in the Old Testament. And Paul speaks of Christ as one who "did not count equality with God a thing to be grasped," and having been obedient to death on the cross, he is now exalted by God and glorified so that at the name of Jesus every tongue should confess that "Jesus Christ is Lord, to the glory of God the Father."[20]

What is of major importance is that radical faith finds God laying Himself open to man in a distinctive way in Christ. By the deep intimacy of Jesus' fellowship with the Father, by his obedience and fidelity as the Servant of the Most High—a role which Jesus himself appears increasingly to have assumed consciously—and by the love which takes him even to the cross, God strikes home to the heart of man. By this man He establishes our existence in faith, and by that act enables us to live with Him continuously as our Creator, Judge, and Redeemer.

No note rings more persistently in Jesus' life and teaching than the sovereignty of God. His kingly yet loving rule directs and sustains His entire creation. "He makes his sun rise on the evil and the good, and sends rain on the just and unjust."[21] He stands in a deeper connection with man than that of a giver of moral laws. Not only the righteous but the unrighteous are recipients of existence at His hands. Material prosperity and good fortune are not then to be mistaken for tokens of the divine preference for individuals or nations. There is a kind of splendid "indifference" or equanimity on God's part which bestows life upon creatures of all kinds, even upon those who defy His rule and deny His love. However, it is an "indifference" also to those fallible human judgments which would proportion earthly goods on the condition of virtue or its lack. God reserves to Himself the ultimate judgment to which men are not privy. He remains the Lord, upholding all, not because they are "good" or in spite of their "evil," but because they are His. His love, exhibited in the giving of existence itself, cannot be twisted into a conditional act dependent upon our spiritual and moral attainment. And it is this conviction out of which springs Christ's love for men. They are simply given to him as from the hand of God. In his concern for the outcast, the poor, the unrighteous, the diseased and maimed, Christ reveals a God who does not cast off His creation but ceaselessly moves to its redemption.

Here then, in the last analysis, is not "indifference" but a goodness so bountiful that it reaches beyond moral requirements to the acceptance of the persons themselves. In this respect the love of God seen in Christ may be likened, if only brokenly, to that of loving parents for their children. It is impossible for parents to say which of their several children they love most. Each is loved in a distinctive way, yet all of them are loved simply because they exist. The children are not loved because they are smart, cute, handy around the house, or docile. Their very existence is the focus of parental love. When they are dirty, quarrelsome, unforgiving, when they get into trouble and in every ordinary sense become quite unlovable, parental love still puts the food on the table, furnishes clothes, provides for education and health to the best of its ability. Parental distress does not destroy the love and care in which the children in a real sense live. This does not mean that responsible parents do nothing about the children's shortcomings, but it first of all means that there is a deeper level of relation between parent and child than that of the moral, and this is an unconditional relation of concern for the child's existence. When the child is dangerously ill, parental love does not spend time lecturing him on thumb-sucking or getting his feet wet. It concentrates on his life, and the parent anxiously seeks his recovery.

On an immeasurably vaster scale Christ teaches and lives in the providential care of God. We see God in him, first of all as the Father and King of the entire family of man, the One in whom we are invited to trust as the dependable ground of our being.

In Christ, Christian faith sees God as Judge and Redeemer, the power of righteousness thrust against the evil of the world, and the power of sacrificial love wooing it to a new integrity in communion with Him. We have noticed in part how God judges us in Christ by revealing to us our nature and need. But what from the beginning struck Christian faith as the summit of Christ's work is the redemptive love of God which illuminates it all. Paul's words remain the center of the Christian hope: "All this is from God, who through Christ reconciled us to himself and gave us the ministry of reconciliation; that is, in Christ God was reconciling the world to himself."[22]

Christ consorted with people of all kinds. He identified himself with those who, to all intents and purposes, were worthless, as well as those who were decent and plied respectable vocations. But the major impress, as opposition to him showed, was his concern for the outcast, the unrighteous, the lost.[23] He not only told of the Good Samaritan, the lost coin and sheep, the Prodigal Son, but he actually accepted the woman who was a sinner, chose a despised tax collector for a companion, appeared regularly with those outside the pale of orthodox piety, and died between two thieves. He seemed supremely careless of his own reputation, so long as the needy were helped. He redeemed them from fearful isolation, moral shoddiness and worthlessness by throwing about them the mantle of forgiving love. He drew them out of themselves into the fellowship of repentant obedience to the divine will. "Here are my mother and my brothers! Whoever does the will of God is my brother and sister and mother."[24] As Tillich puts it, "He accepted the unacceptable," and by this act was their redemption begun and God's love evidenced.[25]

It was not only his teaching and life which revealed the yearning love of God for human reconciliation. For Christian faith, the climax of the drama comes with the Crucifixion and the Resurrection. In these acts Christian faith continues to see the love which accepts, which suffers to accept, and the triumph of that love over death itself.

The Cross is not a strategy of social reform. Nor does it prove that suffering love always in measurable time wins over brutality and evil. In worldly terms, it failed. Neither is it a method carefully calculated to outflank the calloused hearts of those who win their ways by guile or oppression. It is not a desperate expedient, recklessly snatched at in order to secure followers—as though Christ died with one eye on prospective disciples! The Cross is not a bloody sacrifice offered on man's behalf to an offended deity whose mind would thereby be changed from hate to love for humanity. So Richard Baxter put it: "Christ came not into the world to make

God better, but to make us better. Nor did He die to make God more disposed to do good, but to dispose us to receive it. . . ."[26] It is not offended majesty, but broken love offered to unworthiness, of which the Cross speaks. And that is not simply the love of one man for his fellows, but the love of God in one man reaching out to all men. "When the early Christians looked back and pondered on the dreadful thing that had happened, it made them think . . . not simply of the love of Jesus, but of the love of God."[27] Out of the wonder of that conviction, Paul cries, "God shows his love for us in that while we were yet sinners Christ died for us."[28]

In Christ's death we may see a love so unconditional that its offering is not contingent upon our acceptance of it, a love which did not cease at the limit of man-made death. Only such a love can redeem us, for it puts us "outside" the framework of our self-regarding interests and sets us before a love to the uttermost. Only a love which is free can save us from bondage. Only a love which suffers, showing the unutterable pain which our sin effects in the Father, can break the fatal fascination with which our sinfulness continues to lure us into slavery. The love of the Cross is such a love, unveiled in human agony, but in perfect faithfulness to Him who is faithful above all others. As God calls Christ to Himself through death, the trusting love of Christ, by which he passed through death, becomes to us the very love which calls Christ to itself. It is the love of God manifested in Christ.

Regarded as a historical fact, the Crucifixion may not evoke or establish faith. It may be said that death had the final say, as it always does, about every fine thing in human experience. The Crucifixion could as well be the flat contradiction of a belief in God's love as its confirmation. However, the Cross is not self-explanatory, and this the early Christians well knew. For them the Crucifixion and the Resurrection were firmly bound together into one tremendous act of revelation. The apparent finality and futility of the Cross receives its resounding reply in Christ's being raised from the dead. The Cross reveals divine love when it is seen from beyond itself in the light of the living Christ.

Insuperable difficulties block any attempts to reconstruct the precise nature of the Resurrection. The typical question, "What actually happened?" can probably never be satisfactorily stated in physical or psychological terms.[29] What actually happened was not in the realm of sensible phenomena, any more than was Paul's Damascus road experience, but it had to be stated in sense-bound phrases to communicate its powerful impact. It is surprising that the gospels do not regard belief in the risen Christ as springing from the empty tomb. The words of the young man by the tomb, the angels, or Peter, even the first appearances of Christ produce instead astonishment and disbelief. Yet dismay gives way to confidence and hope during the repeated appearances of the Lord. The disciples meet him as the living Christ, the one who is not dead but an immediately apprehended presence among them. In whatever form this transformative event took place, it is clear that the disciples recognized a continuity between the Master with whom they had trudged the Galilean roads and their Risen Lord.[30] He was not, as risen, a figment, but as real to them as the "spirit" we feel in a closely knit group under the stress of some crucial occurrence. "The situation in the early church," we agree with Professor Knox, "was not that Jesus was believed to be living because he was believed to have risen; it was rather that he was known to have risen because he was known as living."[31]

Contrary to all expectation and with a vividness which was completely convincing, Christ lived and moved among the living. His obedience unto the Cross had been crowned not with death but with life, and thereby was opened a new dimension of life for those who had felt and continued to sense the impact of his presence. The Resurrection was and continues to be one of those life-changing meetings of being with being from which stream hope, purification, and fresh energy. It is not first of all a doctrine but an actual engagement by which the character of the experient is radically altered. The Christian faith established in this act of God emerged convinced that God had shown Himself in power by raising Christ from the dead, thereby certifying him as the "chosen one," the church's Lord. Death and evil had not proved unconquerable for God's love. They had not been able to deflect it by brutality, insensitiveness, or disbelief. Rather, these had been turned wrong side out and changed into a means of glorification of God's mercy and judgment. The love of God was indeed bent on reconciling the world to Himself, and there could be no final blockage of His purpose. The risen Christ was the seal of the promised reconciliation in which the despair of loneliness and sin would themselves be destroyed, as even now they were for the first Christians.

In all truth which touches the depth of one's existence there is a formidable ultimacy. It takes over the person's life by its inescapable absoluteness, not by its claim to universal acceptance. It is truth because it forms the character of the self in terms of which all lesser ideas are adjudged to be true or false. No referendum of popular or learned opinion is awaited. About such truth there is something of the immediacy of self-consciousness which refuses to be argued out of court. It has become the standpoint from which all arguments are estimated. Christ, his teaching, life, cross, resurrection, and continuing presence thus intrude into our personal histories, laying ground for our interpretations of ourselves, the world, and God Himself. He is the Christ for those to whom he opens life in faith.

All that saw him in life and heard him were not so persuaded. For many he simply was not the double revealer of man and God. His name virtually disappeared among his own people; Judaism was not inwardly reformed by his coming, and it remained for a mixed group of Jews and Gentiles to exalt him above all earthly rulers and authorities. He was not the Christ for all, nor is he today.

There are those, however, to this day whose faith finds in him its direction and hope. He is for them the Way, the Truth, and the Life. They cannot prove by argument that he is Lord of Lords; they can but witness to the reality which has grasped them through him, and gratefully respond in a life of loving service to Him who by Christ grants recourse from despair and illumination of the mystery of existence itself.

IV

Faith and God, Its Ultimate Object

None of us lives to himself, and none of us dies to himself. If we live, we live to the Lord, and if we die, we die to the Lord; so then, whether we live or whether we die, we are the Lord's. [Romans 14:7-8]

And one called to another and said,
"Holy, holy, holy is the Lord of hosts;
the whole earth is full of his glory."
And I said: "Woe is me! for I am lost; for I am a man of unclean lips, and I dwell in the midst of a people of unclean lips; for my eyes have seen the King, the Lord of Hosts!" [Isaiah 6:3, 5]

Behold the dwelling of God is with men. He will dwell with them, and they shall be his people. . . . I am the Alpha and Omega, the beginning and the end. To the thirsty I will give water without price from the fountain of the water of life. [Revelation 21:3, 6; 22:5]

Now to him who is able to keep you from falling and to present you without blemish before the presence of his glory with rejoicing, to the only God, our Savior through Jesus Christ our Lord, be glory, majesty, dominion, and authority before all time and now and for ever. Amen. [Jude 24-25]

IN OUR casual use of the words "faith" and "belief" we reveal the underlying pattern of faith. We assume there must be two entities at least, a self, who trusts, and an object of some kind, in which this trust comes to rest. If the self does not recognize or hold as worthful a potential object, clearly no question of faith is involved. If the subject and object are supposed to be identical, there is no faith, because significant relations of belief are impossible. There must be crucial differences in the character of the two for faith to exist, but there must also be some bond of connection between them which permits them to be considered together in a unity. Whatever else this connecting bond is, it includes the notion that the object is in some sense "real," "genuine," and over against the subject. Thus when we seriously use such expressions as "I trust that man," "I believe in democracy," "I have faith in God," or even "I believe in myself," we assume that these objects are "there," confronting us in their own right, and that they are not as objects merely derivative from ourselves. They are irreducibly "real" objects or "authentic" possibilities. To be in faith seems then to mean, at a minimum, that we find ourselves confronted by an impelling and powerful datum which we do not create or invent.[1] Although to an outsider this sense of objectivity may seem the veriest nonsense or the height of self-deception, to the subject involved, faith would be impossible without this commandingly real and worthful object.

In radical Christian faith, as we have pointed out, the ultimate object of faith is not Jesus Christ himself. Rather Christ pointed beyond himself to a still deeper ground, as he strove in obedient trust with his destiny. We also recognize that for ourselves there is an ultimate object beyond Christ, because the possibility of Jesus' being the Christ for us lay neither in him nor in ourselves, but in the power by which it was given to us to accept him as Lord. Our task then is to spell out in whatever degree is possible the nature of the engagement of the self with the Ultimate Object, God.

As we proceed to this task, however, we find our path blocked by a variety of faiths, all of which proclaim they are "true" faiths. Each, at first blush, seems to have the polar form of faith. It claims to trust or believe in something outside the self's capacity for immediate achievement. The something to which it cleaves stands over against the self as real in some sense, and it offers guidance and purposive fulfillment. As we look about us, it becomes distressingly plain that men do take comfort and hope from a wide assortment of objects: power, prestige, sex, wealth, health, the state, reason, pleasure, religious faith, the family. In one way or another, it is maintained, these objects will bring one through the vicissitudes of life without recourse to God.

The natural question then arises, "Can we not invent or select any one or a combination of such objects and, by giving ourselves to their pursuit, invest our lives with purpose and zest?" "After all," the question intimates, "isn't faith a purely subjective affair, the creation of human desires, reason, appetites, and hopes?" Man alone makes and breaks the gods. He gives or withholds allegiance. He may believe in whatsoever suits his fancy or fits the strongest motives of the moment. The choice of objects is his, and all that seems necessary is that the objects of faith *appear* to be objects, not figments of the imagination. Whatever objectivity there is to the goals of human desire and trust lies within the range of the subjects' psychological structure. The subject is at root the disposer of its objects, even to the degree of formulating them as objects to the mind!

It would seem necessary for a radical faith to take seriously this subjective attitude toward faith and to examine its implications. Admittedly, the subjective attitude commends itself to us at first because it appears to describe with reasonable accuracy what we actually do. We find it agreeable to rest back on a theory which in a general way sheds light on our behavior. Even more important to its widespread acceptance is the way it ministers to our deep desire for domination over our existence and our yearning for freedom from all external constraint. It leaves man at the center of the total picture comfortable in his assumed sovereignty, disposing his loyalty where and when he pleases. Even God becomes one among an almost limitless number of possibilities to which we might assign our faith. We shall decide, as men have done before us, what notion of God shall please us or offend us. Man alone dominates the ends for which he lives.

However, human autonomy as represented in this subjective view of faith cannot be purchased by deflating existence to the dimensions of human desire and imagination. The charge of wishful thinking, customarily made against theistic faith, may be as readily hurled at the subjectivists. They may have saved the appearance of autonomy by a limited or faulty analysis of the human situation.

The objects in which men trust may be diverse, but there remains the impressive fact of primal faith. Men may in freedom choose their gods—this, Christian faith has no interest in denying; but they do not choose to choose, choose to be free, or decide to have faith. From the beginning man is set as a dependent and finite being in some faith relation, and, at least in this case, he does not dispose of his faith to imaginary or finite objects but to the factual and inescapable power of being in which he participates by virtue of his existing at all. As a common humanity we have been given a situation as real as any we are likely to meet. It is one of a subject-object polarity in which we cannot, without denying our existence, deny the reality of the object which exercises determinative power over us. We cannot clearly and in detail specify the characteristics of this object from the standpoint of primal faith. We can know it is there as actually objective. We know we are dependent upon it and that we are called upon to take some attitude of defiance, indifference, or trust toward it. But we cannot wish it away or deny its presence. Our limitations and finitude speak so loudly that our words cannot be heard.

The subjective understanding of faith, interestingly enough, accepts this inevitability of faith as a kind of psychological presupposition for its own position. Unfortunately it fails to reckon with the implications of this situation as pointing toward some inclusive and ultimate object of trust which is not at the mercy of human disposal. Yet the universal testimony to the need itself for some ultimate object of trust is part of the evidence which must be taken into account by the subjectivist reading of faith. The insatiable, deep-seated hunger of the self to come up against the ultimate—even though we grant for the moment that it is never satisfied in this world—looks toward the possibility of overcoming the incoherencies and erratic partialities of our lesser faiths. The yearning of the self for release from the inner contradictions in which these faiths embroil him cannot be dismissed as though it shed no light on the human situation. It may suggest the unworthiness of any faith which magnifies the finite into an absolute.

Hence a Christian understanding of faith challenges the idea that finite objects really can and do profoundly and inclusively command human trust. Even when lesser objects seriously engage our fidelity, do they not point beyond themselves to a unity and inclusiveness which they cannot encompass? In the fervid pursuit of sex satisfaction, financial gain, rational order, or religious practices, we are aware that no one of these fills or can even hope to fill the whole horizon of life. We cannot organize all life about them. Nor can we work out a combination of them as our object of ultimate loyalty, for they get into each other's ways in the most painful and disturbing fashion. Even when they do claim universal sway, they pay grudging tribute to the deeper, universal being in which they are grounded, and by participation in which they appeal to us, at least for the moment, as offering universality. Their appearance of universality, as well as our apparent freedom, is but the broken image of God's universal sway and the freedom which He wills for His human creation. But no one of our finite faiths does actually unify the shifting, turbulent stream of experience for more than a passing moment. No one of them sits triumphant for very long on the prostrate body of its competitor. No one of them, when pressed to the extreme, but backfires into revulsion, or constrains human life into ever-narrowing appreciations and service. No one of them but sooner or later dies—not at the end of our life but in its middle, when conviction crumples before doubt and hope droops into despair. So the spirit of man transcends even his own self-chosen goals and seeks assuagement in a deeper reality than finite loyalties ever touch. He knows at root that they are but extensions of himself, that, although often they bear his high hopes, they are riddled with self-will and fruitless passion, and that they never rise higher than their source in a free but anxiety-ridden self.

The subjective interpretation of faith is merely a variation on the Biblical theme of "idolatry," and it is "idolatry" far more than agnosticism or atheism with which radical faith has to deal in each of us. We must have our treasured gods or go mad or die. We must substitute the finite, tangible, sensible for the infinite and unseen. We must attribute absolute dominion or authority to some favorite fragment of experience, making of it our idol. But no idol ever fell before argument or scoffing; only repeated tough experience itself can gnaw away at its base. We know how to dodge and protect ourselves from each other, but the constant erosion of one after the other of our idolatries is the sign that something deeper and more skillful than human ingenuity is at work. He whom Francis Thompson called the "Hound of Heaven" is the enemy we cannot ultimately evade. What Unamuno named "the suffocation of the spirit" becomes unbearable, and we are thrust out of our isolated strongholds in "vital anguish" to try our fate with Him.[2] To that crucial encounter we must now turn.

By way of introduction to this difficult act of confession, perhaps the perspective within which to describe the meeting of God and man should be laid out. Of late it has become customary to speak of this encounter in the terms of Martin Buber's category of the I-Thou relation. The subject-object relation, it is said, is not only inadequate but false to the dramatic and personal quality of the event. Thus, for example, Emil Brunner holds that a category "of an entirely different kind" must be used, that of the I-Thou. The subject-object relation he finds "un-Biblical" as it takes an impersonalistic view of God, thereby denying His initiatory power. It culminates in "objectivism," by which he means "a tendency of man's spirit and will to get something into his power . . . something which by its very nature is not under human control."[3] On the other hand, the I-Thou relation is one in which God as an I addresses man as Thou, and man as I addresses God as Thou. In this experience is born "a relation of personal correspondence."[4] In the same vein, Herberg describes this event as "an immediate self-validating encounter which transcends the ordinary distinction between subject and object, just as does any genuine encounter between man and man."[5] Thus the personal category is presumed to be the only form in which a meeting of God and man can be even approximately expressed. Buber himself states the issue succinctly: "God can never become an object for me; I can attain no other relation to Him than that of the I to its eternal Thou, that of the Thou to its eternal I." Or again, "The eternal Thou can by its nature not become It."[6]

Buber's words are strong ones—indeed, they are too strong! Unquestionably much of our engagement with God must be couched in terms of I-Thou, especially when we attempt to confess what is happening to us. Therefore modern theology is put in heavy debt to this great Jewish thinker for his illuminating and subtle exposition of man's situation before God. There are, however, some decisive limitations in his position which should be recognized before we are swept along to the highly dubious conclusion that this I-Thou relation has replaced the subject-object relation in virtually all areas of knowledge.

It is somewhat breath-taking to be told that "the eternal Thou can by its very nature not become It." In this assertion we seem to be told categorically that the uniqueness of the divine must conform to personalistic categories, as though He had relinquished that sovereignty and freedom by which He meets us how He wills. Either the deity is limited by prescribing at the outset that He must conform to the I-Thou relation which we find operative on the purely human level, or, by means of some superior insight into the "nature" of God, we are apprised of an inward rigidity or limitation of His very character. The former alternative suggests a high-handed translation of categories from the personal and human level to the level of the divine in its full uniqueness. The latter alternative represents a denial of His sovereignty and, it may be, the authenticity of the experiences of those who simply do not meet God in this fashion. The power, majesty, holiness of God, which call for categories that are transpersonal, simply do not come to some people by the route of the I-Thou. Austin Farrer, writing in a disparaging vein, tells of having unsuccessfully attempted to establish an I-Thou dialogue with God. He concludes, "And this is why when Germans set their eyeballs and pronounce the terrific words, 'He speaks to thee' [*Er redet dich an*] I am sure, indeed, that they are saying something but I am still more sure that they are not speaking to my condition."[7] Perhaps Whitehead's comment that a personal God is "an inference and not a direct intuition" even for Christianity should be taken seriously.[8]

There are those points in the human engagement with God when the superpersonal power of the deity is so overwhelming that personal categories cannot bear the weight of meaning. As Whitehead put it, He is the Void and the Enemy as well as the Friend, and He may at different times and circumstances be all of them to us. Our faith, in one aspect, is not a dialogue with a gracious Thou or even a sternly demanding Thou. It consists rather in waiting in the dark before an overpowering and solemn mystery which denies all nearer approach. God is there, but hidden in the recesses of the Void, in the Nothingness from which no word issues. Yet we are bound to the Void; it is a reality very few escape. Or again, the splendor of the divine majesty breaks forth upon us, striking us silent or lifting us up in exultation and praise whether He, It, or other persons hear.

Rudolph Otto's recognition of this form of religious experience led him to point out that "Third person hymns are not necessarily less, but under certain conditions may even be more genuine and first hand utterances than those which address God as 'Thou.' . . . It is often thought," he continued, "that designations of deity in impersonal neuter terms ('It') rather than in terms of person and masculine pronoun . . . are too poor and too pale to gain a place in our Christian thought of God. But this is not always correct.

Frequently such terms indicate the mysterious overplus of the non-rational and numinous, that cannot enter our 'concepts' because it is too great and too alien to them. . . ."[9] Not even the Biblical view of God consistently holds to the personalistic or second-person categories. There are those moments when the power of the spirit comes upon men with force, and the rubrics of the personal fail to bear the weight placed upon them.[10] The holiness of God may bear us down in a creatureliness or elevate us to ecstatic heights, and then we worship Him or It with ejaculations of "Alleluia" or "Holy, Holy, Holy"—not with personal discourse or propositions.

The fervor with which Buber's concept of the I-Thou has been embraced is understandable. It points to one of the profoundest aspects of the meeting of God and man. It represents a legitimate reaction against those forms of religious thought which treat God as a passive entity awaiting man's discovery and inspection. The term "object" has become a foil of criticism precisely because it is assumed that it derives solely from the pattern of scientific knowledge in which the specimen simply awaits the action of the investigator. In part, the difficulty also arises from the fact that the English language uses one word, "object," for two distinct meanings in the German, the language in which the "I-Thou" has been developed. The term *"Objekt"* usually signifies an impassive entity before a knower, as in the natural sciences, whereas the term *"Gegenstand"* more broadly means whatever stands over against another, without determination as to its activity or passivity.[11] The latter meaning is not derivative from the knowledge relation but descriptive of the human situation as such. As Jaspers points out, the dichotomy of the subject-object "cannot be talked out of existence; it can only be understood."[12]

We need not quibble about the use of the word "object." It is probably no more or less adequate than other terms we might employ. But we ought to recognize that the subject-object relation in our context refers essentially to our existence, not to our knowledge. It is the immediately intuited distinction we observe, as beings are over against each other. It stems from the recognition of our limits as persons, our inability to dispose of other beings or to assimilate them into our consciousness. They must be taken account of in their own right. They pronounce their reality by frustrating us in their power to be what they are. They influence us in various

ways and to different degrees and by this action establish themselves as being "there" and not "here" in us.[13]

It appears to us that our situation in faith is of this subject-object
character. God stands over against us as that unique Object who
lies outside the range of human control and disposition, yet who
enters into effective relations with us. He wills to meet us in His
own authenticity in whatever manner and time He pleases. We
cannot, therefore, determine in advance of our personal encounter
with Him what form this encounter must assume for us. Even as
the advocates of the I-Thou relation cannot determine for us the
way in which we shall be met of God, neither can we determine
for them. But we do not feel justified in deducing a notion of His
character from a theory of knowledge, whether it be of a scientific
or of a personalistic type.[14] We can only hope to insure that the
way of faith be construed in such a manner as to give opportunity
for the expression of the unique nature of deity, whether it turns
out to be expressible in the third- or second-person, personal or transpersonal categories of our language. It remains for faith to report,
as we have done, that God is Object in the sense that He is not
merely a construct or a discovery of the human mind, and that He
does stand over against us as the ultimately real, with which we have
the most serious business to transact.[15]

When we turn to speak confessionally of this encounter with the
Ultimate Object, we are bewildered by our first impression of disorder. Everything may seem to be happening at the same time.
Insights and changes swiftly transpire in the depths of the self
before we can grasp their meaning. Our natural tendency may be
to bring order out of this chaos by looking back to discern definite
steps by which it has come upon us. Or we commence to devise
schemes of logical and temporal sequence for our description of it.
We may even snatch at certain features of the total experience, such
as hope, trust, confidence, knowledge, love, etc., and identify them
as the essence of faith. Yet all this apparent disarray and confusion
is what one might have expected. If faith is a continuing confrontation initiated by a living Lord, not an inert principle, if we are
not part of the divine and therefore are excluded from the depth
of its purposes, if we are by nature subject to ceaseless growth and
change, and if God calls each of us to stand for himself, then each
man's meeting with God will strike him as a unique process to
which general principles do not apply, especially if they be drawn

from alien experiences. Yet in certain respects faith is like a battle, the pattern whereof emerges during the battle itself and is not imposed upon it from without. And, as in the thick of battle we are not aware of a foreordained victory, so in faith we fail to discover the ultimate resolution within a specifiable historical period.[16] Faith thus must be understood as the total ongoing event of living before the God of Jesus Christ, and the pattern which develops with it. For each person there are sources of unique meaning which may not be exactly repeated in the experience of another. Yet we are prevented from slipping off into private anarchy because these meanings when carefully and fully reported in an open manner may show up resemblances among our diverse experiences. When we cross-check them for correction and amplification, as faith in God calls us to do as rational beings and members one of another, there is more order than at first appears. We recognize then that it is the same God who deals with each of us even if in each case there remains the precious uniqueness of our own experience. If for one the engagement of faith is a slow development in peace and serenity, the note of compelling judgment is never totally absent; if for another faith is an agonizing conflict with deity, the note of assurance and quietude is never completely stilled.

From the standpoint of faith God is both the fulfiller and the transformer of human existence. At one and the same time we discover Him to be the One upon whom we can confidently rest our lives and yet the One who contradicts and challenges our lives. He makes our former imaginations look childish and unworthy while He summons us to accept and trust Him for new hopes implanted on the rubbish heaps of the old. He brings us to trust Him even when we fail to comprehend Him with our minds and hearts. We continue to doubt Him even while we know ourselves to be inextricably bound to His love and patience. He draws us to Himself but checks us from easy familiarity by His power and righteousness, so far beyond our own. He gives us freedom to "talk back" to Him but reminds us that our rejoinders and criticisms are uttered in His presence. So He fulfills our destiny while showing us how our destinies are changed in His hands. He may be the "no" to our "yes," the "yes" to our "no," but He is also the "yes" to our "yes," the "no" to our "no" as our lives move increasingly into the orbit of His faithfulness toward us.

Then may faith see Him as the love which knits together in unity and order the potential disorders of the realms of nature and humanity. He is the mercy which stoops beside the broken of body and spirit, the strength which, welling up unbidden, lifts the weakest and comforts the forlorn. To the proud, He is the invincible enemy, working to their ruin; to the righteous, the questioner of their virtue; to the learned, the remembrance of their ignorance and conceit; to the brave, the image of their furtive cowardice. But to the meek He gives confidence; to the unrighteous, forgiveness and fresh beginnings; to the foolish, wisdom; and upon the coward He confers the bravery to go on in spite of fear. He meets us as the paradox, the contradiction of every premature truth and self-sufficient virtue, the affirmation of every impulse and act which brings deeper communion among men and between men and Himself.

Through it all, faith recognizes God as the One whose ways are not our ways, who remains as the Object supreme over against us, from whose hands none escapes unscathed. George Herbert expresses in this vein the tension in which the man of faith lives:

> Lord, Thou didst make me, yet Thou woundest me;
> Lord, Thou dost wound me, yet Thou dost relieve me;
> Lord, Thou relievest, yet I die by Thee!
> Lord, Thou dost kill me, yet Thou dost reprieve me.
> I cannot skill of these Thy ways.[17]

Confronted with a situation in which we find ourselves constantly "off balance" before God, it is no wonder that many conceive the encounter with God as a wrestling or a battle. Faith, for them, comes at first not as a facile alleviation of doubt and an easy way out to peace but as a tremendous conflict with their destiny.[18] They cannot gradually sidle closer to deity; they must taste the depth of despair in the meaningless, and then leap, to use Kierkegaard's word, beyond the abyss of absurdity which surrounds them to the "whatever" is on the other side. And if they "land" or are "caught" on the other side, the battle is still before them, with the significant difference that they know it must be fought on the ground and by the power which He Himself provides. Despair is not conquered in one gigantic affirmation. Life continues with its pressures, frustrations, and abiding sorrows, but at least the Enemy has been identified, and the ground rules for the ensuing battle have been drawn. The issues of life and death have been cast in a new dimension. Now it must be lived in full self-awareness, face to face with Him.

Jeremiah knows himself to be before God; nevertheless he calls Him a deceiver, one who has made a fool of him before men. God is trustworthy to the extent that He is present unfailingly, but this does not comfort Jeremiah. Instead, to him God is likened to a "deceitful brook," "waters that fail." Yet the prophet cries out,

> If I say, "I will not mention him, or speak any more in his name,"
> There is in my heart as it were a burning fire shut up in my bones,
> And I am weary with holding it in, and I cannot.[19]

Jesus meets God in Gethsemane as the one who stands over against Him and wrestles in prayer with his moot destiny until the words of submission come.[20] From the cross the cry of dereliction is wrung from him in agony and accusation, yet it is a cry not of disbelief or unfaithfulness. It is the cry of a man who knows God is there in the darkness, and whose torment would be the less if there were no God to whom to appeal. The battle is the harder to sustain as long as God is present; without Him there is no problem of suffering and meaning. To both Jeremiah and Jesus, God is the Enemy, but He is a curious type of enemy, unknown in the world, who claims their trust in the very moment of forsaking, who is present to them as the inescapable reality when all else except suffering goes out of focus and becomes unreal.[21] They are His and He has chosen to meet them in His own way.

The cases of Jeremiah and Jesus are not totally unlike those of other men. We find that agony accompanies the shift of gravity from our own center to that of the divine ground. Our cherished self-centered convictions stave off the assault of the divine power. We do not want to have the image of ourselves and our place in the world knocked askew by the realization that we are not centers of independent authority, that only God is worthy of worship. We desire the shelter of our private world with its skillfully wrought defenses. Yet strangely enough we dimly sense that we are already known through and through. The secrets of the deepest self are already laid bare; we only lack the courage to accept the verdict. So when the breach in the walls of self comes, it arrives both as an assault and as a relief column. His love comes as conqueror, but also as a long-awaited support for those forces which have been at work undermining self-righteousness and pride. We may at last stand in commitment, naked and alone before His majesty and grace, but we will be heartily joyous that our Captor is such a one as will forgive us our defiance. Faith is the struggle, but it is also the surrender, the assent to Him who has driven us from our last refuge. He has revealed Himself as our rightful Master, and no longer need we cower behind our manifold subterfuges. The entire scene is illuminated because of His revelation by which we have been apprehended.[22] And perhaps after the struggle, or even during it, we have the intimation that all that has happened is not the product of our efforts for commitment and surrender, or our attempts to escape the moment of decision. What we realize is the presence of a gift whose giving we could not hasten or defer by our strenuous actions. The break-through came, we at last admit, not by our own devising, but from a graciousness which knew what we needed before ever we desired it.[23] A new existence has been set in motion which we can but accept wherever it may lead.[24]

No single term adequately embraces the manifold facets of this new condition. Paul spoke of the "new creation" in Christ; Jonathan Edwards discoursed about the "new frame of heart or taste" for divine things; Paul Tillich, in our own time, refers to the "new Being." "I do not merely feel changes; I am changed," wrote Forsyth. "There has been what I can only call a new creation, using the strongest word in my reach."[25] In spite of peripheral differences of thought, there is a consensus here. The estate of faith is radical; it runs to the depth of the person; it is total in its impact; it is unconditional and absolute in significance. Furthermore, it is new; no mere rearrangement of the old elements has taken place; unforeseen power has erupted in the midst of one's world. Above all it is not merely a revelation of information, a fresh way of observing familiar experiences and eternal verities. It is first of all a state or process of being which has been bestowed. By the reorientation of the total self, a new way of looking at the self, mankind, nature, and God is possible; a new relation of the parts of existence has occurred. Thus as Tillich says, "Faith is not an opinion, but a state."[26]

One might begin to lay out the nature of this new being by noting that it rectifies the false image we have hitherto held of ourselves. Whereas we were prone to see ourselves, our culture, or our institutions at the center of existence, we now begin to see God as truly Lord, as the center or ground of our existence. He is not relegated to the extreme limits of human life as a conclusion to a long-drawn-out argument which never convinced us; He is here as the One with whom we enter into the most profound communion

The Current Selection

RENEWAL IN RETREATS

by John L. Casteel

The rapid growth among Protestants of the practice of holding retreats has been a phenomenon of recent years, and in this book a leader who has proved exceptionally helpful to ministers in conducting such retreats tells how and why it is done.

A PHRASE which is beginning to be used in Protestant circles—"to make retreat"—indicates a new interest. Until recently one seldom heard the term. Today there are churches in which "retreats" for groups of members have become a recognized part of its program for training in the spiritual life.

The retreat is a means of securing detachment from the hustle and bustle of the world in order to get one's bearings again and to renew life at its fountainhead. In this new book a leader who has proved exceptionally helpful to ministers in conducting such retreats tells how and why it is done.

The book is primarily a practical manual of methods. It shows just how to proceed, step by step, in projecting a retreat, in interesting the right people in attending, in arranging for the most favorable physical setting, in planning the living arrangements, in developing the program. It even covers such detailed matters as the number to be invited, the duration of the retreat, a time schedule for every part of the day, the use to be made of silence, the place of a period of physical work, whether to celebrate the Holy Communion or not.

Behind these specific plans lies a clear conception of what a retreat is and is designed to do. The practices which are suggested are rooted in a fundamental understanding of the nature of Christian experience. In arriving at this under-

Excerpts from
RENEWAL IN RETREATS

"We are all victims of the acceleration of life today. The peril of personal and social disintegration that results can be overcome only through the recovery of the practice of disciplined introversion. The function of retreat is to provide for that interior retirement, in which the self can come to know both the conscious and the unconscious sources of its being."

"Most people today have never had any genuine experience of keeping silent for a sustained period. The prospect of having to keep still for more than an Armistice Day's One Minute of Silent Tribute threatens the precarious balance of nerves and activity by which they manage to keep going in a world of constant noise."

"The retreat will provide amply for solitude. This provision will need to be balanced with due opportunity for participation in the communal life. But the need and the right of each retreatant to freedom from the demands of making himself part of the company, in order that he may enter into solitary communion with God and reflection upon himself, must be taken most responsibly."

"In whatever way the Bible enters into the retreat, the purpose is . . . to read and meditate on the Bible as a means through which we are led into active communion with God, and thereby into deeper fellowship with one another and into surer knowledge of self."

"The actions of a retreat should follow a rhythm of alternation. Certain actions such as joining in worship, engaging in prayer, and taking a hand in the work to be done, call for the retreatant to concentrate and energize his participation. Others, such as resting, reading meditatively . . . invite an attitude of openness, waiting, and relaxation. The alternation should be between active participation and passive receptivity."

standing the author has laid hold of diverse assets. He draws richly on the insights of acknowledged masters of the devotional life, both ancient and modern, like Brother Lawrence, Ignatius Loyola, Baron von Hügel, Evelyn Underhill, Dietrich Bonhoeffer, and Douglas Steere. He takes account of what has been learned by contemporary psychologists about the human personality. He benefits most from his own intensive study of the significance of prayer.

The central purpose of a retreat, as described by Professor Casteel, is the deepening of communion with God. It is thus different from all other types of gettogethers, such as those for study, for inspirational addresses, or for discussion of social problems. The communion with God, however, as interpreted here, involves both a deeper understanding of oneself and community with other persons in Christ.

Until he was forty years old John L. Casteel was a layman, his professional work being in the field of training for effective public speech. In 1942, as a result of his own Christian experience and his deepening contacts with the Church, he was ordained to the Congregational ministry. Today he is professor of pastoral theology and director of field work at the Union Theological Seminary in New York.

In recent years Dr. Casteel has concentrated much of his attention on the devotional life. His "Rediscovering Prayer" has been hailed as the most helpful book on the subject since Fosdick's "Meaning of Prayer." His "Spiritual Renewal Through Personal Groups" is the chief source of information about the experiments of local churches in forming small inner-circles for more dedicated Christian living. As a leader of retreats for many different kinds of groups he has had an especially rich experience, the fruits of which are harvested in his present book.

HELPFUL BOOKS FOR THE MAN IN THE PULPIT

One Dividend Credit given with each book purchased. To order, write title(s) wanted on enclosed card and indicate whether your order is in addition to, or instead of, the current selection.

YOUR MONEY & YOUR CHURCH

By Richard Byfield & James P. Shaw

Two experts in applied stewardship blend financial realism and spiritual insights to show that giving is an integral part of the Christian's commitment. Full of specific, usable suggestions to help the local pastor. $3.95

BEST SERMONS, 1959-60

Edited by G. Paul Butler

This collection of sermons by forty-two Protestant preachers from both here and abroad is a rich mine of homiletical ideas, revealing interests as wide and as deep as the Christian Gospel. $3.95

THE RENEWAL OF HOPE

By Howard Clark Kee

Setting forth the Christian ground for certainty of God's ultimate victory, this book shows that the victory must come through man's response to God's will. Full of suggestiveness for expository preaching. Regular Price $3.50; *Club Price $3.00*

A HANDBOOK FOR CHURCH PUBLIC RELATIONS

By Ralph Stoody

Written from the standpoint of the local church in the local community, this handbook gives an expert's detailed blueprint for effective church public relations. $4.00

THEY MET AT PHILIPPI

By Carroll E. Simcox

An introduction to the mind and heart of St. Paul, using the Philippian letter as a portal into his thought and experience. Regular Price $3.75; *Club Price $3.00*

MORE POWER FOR YOUR CHURCH & BUILDING UP YOUR CONGREGATION

By Willard Pleuthner

A revised, combined edition of Mr. Pleuthner's two best-selling manuals of practical help for ministers, incorporating five chapters of significant new material. Regular Price $3.95; *Club Price $3.50*

SPACE, ATOMS, AND GOD

By Jack Finegan

A clear and timely interpretation of what the Christian faith has to say to an age of nuclear fission and space travel. $3.00

PASTORAL PREACHING

By David C. MacLennan

This book by a lucid preacher and writer is distinctive for the way it relates the role of the preacher directly to the needs of the people among whom he lives. $2.50

PREACHING VALUES IN THE EPISTLES OF PAUL

By Halford Luccock

All the qualities that have made Dr. Luccock a long-time favorite, constantly quoted from the pulpit, are found again in undiminished strength in this, his newest volume for preachers. $3.50

MAKER OF HEAVEN AND EARTH

By Langdon Gilkey

This profound but highly readable interpretation of the Christian doctrine of creation shows how relevant is this doctrine to the deepest human needs of our time. Regular Price $4.50; *Club Price $3.75*

PUBLISHED BY THE PULPIT BOOK CLUB, GREAT NECK, L. I., NEW YORK

1159 Printed in U.S.A.

as subjects, rightly called, before an Ultimate Object. The heavy weight of fretful responsibility we assumed in imagining ourselves fortuitously placed at the focal point of existence is removed by God, to whom it belongs. We do not have to sit up nights to keep the universe running, as someone said. The distorted perspective we have introduced into the world begins to slip back into an ordered pattern. Some of our jumbled relations to others begin to straighten out in meaningful communication.

The familiar threefold pattern of God as Creator, Judge, and Redeemer takes on personal significance to us. Recognizing that we do not originate the energies by which we live, we gratefully accept our existence out of the bounty of His inexhaustible being. Not in our own strength, which is but borrowed strength, but from His, we meet the daily tasks with a power and vigor we formerly simply did not possess. We find it impossible to attribute this rise in energy to our own efforts. We have attempted before to secure it and failed. Nor is it an "explosion" of pent-up powers which in the meantime we had stored within us. Rather it strikes us as unpredictable force, breaking through the habitual structures of our lives, remaking and redirecting as it comes. It grasps us; we do not seize it. Over the abysses of spiritual fatigue, dullness of mind and heart, the despondency of wasted efforts, we are sustained by it. In the presence of the routine and familiar we are charged with a sense of novelty which makes the world itself new. As we are laid hold of by Him and see our ultimate dependence upon Him, we gratefully accept God as the mighty and majestic Creator of our lives and our universe.

However, these energies come upon us in no random and diffuse onrush. Their source is one, the Lord of order, not of tumultuous confusion. He wills His powers to be redemptive, not destructive, to assume patterns of constructive energy within us. As we know ourselves to live from and toward Him, the process of dynamic synthesis takes place. A coherence of the self occurs as we are drawn into a single-minded allegiance to His love which has granted us existence. The internal ruptures of the self are healed; the basic estrangements from ourselves are overcome.[27] Once buffeted about by transient passions and fleeting interests, confused because we did not know how deepest need and most insistent desires could be joined, we now discover a stable pattern developing. The reckless fanaticisms which formerly dissipated our energies for finite ends are brought to a halt in the integrity of the self which arises with faith. "The oneness which the God of Jesus Christ demands in us," declares Richard Niebuhr, "is not the integration of purpose and values, but our integrity, singleness of mind and purity of heart."[28] So does God create in us the channels for effective service by drawing us into a healthy unity of personhood.

Life in the new being is still life under judgment. It is but a response to a righteousness of which ours is a feeble imitation. There is no basis left to us to revel in our virtue when it is placed against the faithfulness of God. We know that no matter how fully we attempt to enter into relations of love and service, there is yet more which could and ought to be done. "The best things we do have somewhat in them to be pardoned," Richard Hooker sagely observed.[29] Ours is a situation of responsibility for the powers committed to us, that they not be used in a slipshod, careless manner. Our moral actions, our religious life and intellectual tasks cannot be left to flow effortlessly, for the sinful propensity still stains them with its self-interest and lethargy. We have not, once and for all, won some stance of commanding pre-eminence, and this we know because God continually impinges upon our lives with new duties to be done, the remembrance of duties left undone.[30] Who ever loves his neighbor as he ought? Who ever loves himself as he ought? Who ever dedicated himself so fully to the eradication of war, racial prejudice, ignorance, and superstition that he could proclaim himself a worthy servant?[31] Who ever exhausted all the possibilities of mutuality in a personal relation? Who is there that can trumpet that he is the captain of his soul, and can make good his boast? Who is there that does not stand in need of forgiveness when his inclinations and the commands of his official position clash, and another is injured by their conflict?

There remains the tension of discontentment in the life of faith, because we stand before His righteousness which is made bearable only by His gracious acceptance of us. The life in the new being is then never one of sloth and ease. We challenge the injustices and evils of our world because He challenges us for our acquiescence and participation in them. We do not pass judgment upon others by a divine authority once and for all delegated to us. We can only judge because He first humbled us by His judgment. We cannot but speak and act when once we have come under his judgment.

Even as we are humbled by His judgment of love, we see in this judgment an act of redeeming love. He would not judge unless He cared enough to judge. His care is seen by His redemption, His acceptance of us into communion with Himself. Creation and judgment are not affairs of a single moment. So redemption and reconciliation are not confined to an instant of our lives. The essence of redemption is a continuing process of reconciliation and acceptance. Knowing ourselves accepted in His presence, we live not fearfully but joyously and soberly, as those who "practice the presence" of God. We can dare to accept ourselves in our shabbiness because He so accepts us. We can accept others, whether or not they confess Him as their Lord, because they are His. As His patience outlasts ours, so does it outlast theirs. The break between man and God is being healed because the love wherewith Christ lived and died came from His side, not our own. The love in which we rejoice has its origin in Him, not ourselves. It has come to us, not we to it. The reconciliation we feel within our own lives has its counterpart in the reconciliation we have with all men through Christ. The love which heals us by uniting us into one being is the love which draws together the family of mankind. The love which suffers yet conquers is God at work in the world, fulfilling His high purpose of communion and fellowship with all men. Faith is the courageous act of living in that love which reunites the severed fragments of one's own life, which integrates the diversity of men into the profoundest communion with each other, and which stands ever open to God's will to communion with man.

Faith is life in communion, but it is not life in union with deity. The distinction between man and God is not obliterated in mystical ecstasy. We are saved in communion and reconciliation with Him; we are not assimilated into a "great sea of being." As we enter into fellowship with God and are accepted in our peculiar uniqueness by Him, we are neither "deified" nor swallowed up in identity with Him. He remains the Ultimate Object, and we, the subjects. In fact, as Aulén has expressed it, "In the realm of faith God is always God and man is always man. The relationship does not pass over into identity.... The closer man comes to God in faith ... the more clearly man becomes aware of that which separates him from God. . . . The consciousness of remoteness . . . is itself a manifestation of God's nearness. . . ."[32] Thus communion and reconciliation do not rule out the sense of the transcendent glory of Him who is worshiped.

Perhaps no word has more often been associated with life in the "new being" than freedom. Certainly it is one of the basic elements in reconciliation by love, because no one can be forced to love God or his fellow man or himself.[33] Paul struck the note of freedom often, as when he called the Galatians to remember that they had been made free from the dietary laws, circumcision, and holidays of the Jewish calendar. "For freedom Christ has set us free," he cried; "stand fast therefore, and do not submit again to a yoke of slavery."[34] Again, when he wrote to the Corinthians, whose moral behavior had become a matter of reproach, he said, "Now the Lord is the Spirit, and where the Spirit is, there is freedom."[35] Yet we find him also warning that this liberty in Christ must not be abused as license.

The life of faith is one of freedom, but freedom is itself paradoxical. It comes to full manifestation only when the self is united by having given itself into bondage to the Ultimate. This is the truth Kierkegaard laid hold of when he said, "If you desire to save it [freedom] and preserve it, there is only one way: in the very second unconditionally and in complete resignation to give it back to God and yourself with it."[36] Only when every lesser attachment is surrendered to the one great original attachment does Christian liberty appear. Only when, as we have previously expressed it, the center of gravity of life is moved from the locus of self to the divine object does the freedom to deal with the subordinate interests and values of life come into proportion. So Emil Brunner takes up the paradox in stating that "Man's freedom springs from the same spot from which comes his dependence. Any attempt to get out of dependence in God leads to slavery."[37] Of course, the point is that freedom is not identical with independence. Rather it is the will to act responsibly toward the power and love of God which is revealed through Jesus Christ; in this it is bound to the nature of a God who Himself loves freely.[38] It is the will to act, unfettered by the impediments of narrow and immediate affections; in this it is freedom and liberty to the full.

The freedom we find in faith is Janus-faced. It is both freedom from and freedom to. It has negative, liberative aspects as well as positive. It is freedom from the clumsy, depressing self-centeredness of sin. It is freedom from the double-mindedness which hampers our full encounter with other persons. It is freedom from the strenuous anxiety and brooding despair about self which robs life of enjoyment.

It is freedom from guilt. It is freedom from striving after God as though He, not we, had been lost. It is freedom from the fragile confidence we repose in men and their institutions, inclusive of religion itself. It is freedom from the moral law, with its burden of duties doggedly carried out. It is freedom from the attractions of sensuality and pride. It is freedom from loneliness. And, at last, it is freedom from the fear of death itself.

Positively, Christian freedom derives from the sovereign God who is Lord freely over His world and word. We are, therefore, free to accept fully everything from His hand. Christian freedom is the freedom to enter into relations with anyone as our neighbor. It is freedom to give ourselves in communion with others. It is freedom to engage in cultural activity—music, art, statesmanship, politics, etc.—without making them into all-engrossing aims. It is the freedom to enjoy the life of the senses, including those of a sexual nature. It is the freedom for the life of the mind, that it can thrust out to explore as far as it pleases. It is the freedom to be oneself, courageously and unashamedly. It is the freedom to be happy. It is the freedom to fulfill the moral law without petty moralism, because we can fulfill it in love. It is the freedom to worship, to think, and to speak. It is the freedom to delight in the sheer abundance of experiences life brings. At last, it is the freedom to worship Him for His own sake by whom all good things are given, the freedom to be wholly at the disposal of God in Christ.

The life of faith issues then in the glorification of God, not for any ulterior motives or "lively hope of favors yet to come." The common utilitarian conception of both faith and God is left behind. As a contemporary Jewish scholar has pointed out, "Religion did not come into existence to console the desperate, to guarantee immortality, or to protect society. It is reality in itself, not a function of man."[39] Here we comprehend the force of Jonathan Edwards' thrust at those who would run to religion and God "not for their own excellent nature, but only to serve a turn."[40]

In the last analysis, faith worships God because He is and because nothing else within man's ken is worthy of supreme and absolute devotion. Yet it is an act of devotion which loves all things in Him, not in depreciation of the precious finite values we cherish. In His majesty, power, glory, love, and justice He stands alone as the first and last object of man's supreme yearning to give himself totally without reserve.

Bernard of Clairvaux traced out the progress of the Christian life many years ago. His pattern may not be the steps by which everyone comes finally to God, but they are identifiable phases of the wrestle with God through which many pass. First, "man loves himself for his own sake; for, he is flesh and he can have no taste for anything except in relation to himself." But realizing "he cannot subsist of himself, he begins to seek God through faith as something, as it were, necessary for him, and to love him." Whereupon he loves God "for his own sake [man's] not for Himself." Again, having found something of God, man passes on to love God "not for his own sake [man's] but for Himself." And beyond this stage Bernard envisions a state in which "man loves himself only for the sake of God," though he admits that in this life this last state "seems impossible."[41]

And perhaps this is the heart of the matter. In loving God for His own sake we are given back to ourselves in a new way. In glorifying Him, not to receive ourselves again, but for His own sake, we may have at least an intimation of what we may become. The God who is loved above all else reveals Himself as the One for whom all creation, inclusive of ourselves, is precious, and we are thus emboldened to love ourselves and all creation for His sake. "For it is impossible for one who loves God not to love himself. For he alone has a proper love for himself who aims diligently at the attainment of the chief and true good; and if this is nothing else but God . . . what is to prevent one who loves God from loving himself?"[42] We therefore owe to Him all honor and glory, in the majestic words of Jude: "Now to him who is able to keep you from falling and to present you without blemish before the presence of his glory with rejoicing, to the only God, our Savior, through Jesus Christ our Lord, be glory, majesty, dominion, and authority, before all time and now and forever. Amen."[43]

Part Two

Christian Faith and the Moral Life

V

Faith and the Ethical Question

For this commandment which I command you this day is not too hard for you, neither is it far off. It is not in heaven, that you should say, "who will go up for us to heaven, and bring it to us, that we may hear it and do it?" . . . But the word is very near you; it is in your mouth and in your heart, so that you can do it. [Deuteronomy 30:11-12, 14[1]]

For I tell you, unless your righteousness exceeds that of the Scribes and Pharisees, you will never enter the Kingdom of heaven. [Matthew 5:20]

I do not understand my own actions. For I do not do what I want, but I do the very thing I hate. . . . For I do not do the good I want, but the evil I do not want is what I do. [Romans 7:15, 19]

Now it is evident that no man is justified before God by the law; for "He who through faith is righteous shall live"; but the law does not rest on faith. . . . [Galatians 3:11-12a]

For freedom Christ has set us free; stand fast therefore, and do not submit again to a yoke of slavery. [Galatians 5:1]

CHRISTIAN faith is concerned about moral conduct for two fundamental reasons. First, because such faith forms the center of personal existence, it operates as the dynamic source of action. Its very nature is to seek irresistibly some form of overt, specific, and responsible expression. Again, because faith is grounded in and directed

79

toward the sovereign God, it recognizes its concern and obedience to be bounded by nothing short of the dimensions of His sway, so far as they can be determined by human insight. Therefore, it is unthinkable for a person of Christian faith to suppose that either his action or his theory of action can be framed without regard to the nature and purposes of God. If no area of being lies outside God's reign, neither can the faith which cleaves to such a deity stop short in practice or theory with some truncated segment of reality, even if it be humanity itself. Morality is then rooted in faith and in the character of the ultimate reality which constitutes the object of faith.

Yet morality in the Western world has been dealt with largely by ethical theorists who have either overlooked or denied its rootage in the religious domain. It has been taken for granted that morality refers only to interhuman relations, and within this perspective the ethical questions have repeatedly been identified and answered. "What is the moral good for man?" "What is morally right for man?" "What values stand pre-eminent as worthy of human effort?" And sometimes, though infrequently, it is asked, "How shall man achieve the moral good, right, or these cherished values?" At first glance, the questions appear to be simple to formulate and apparently win general agreement from ethical philosophers; the diversity of the answers, however, suggests that either the questions are wrongly framed or the human mind is extraordinarily fertile in arriving at variant replies to the same question.[2]

Our task is, first of all, to ascertain the form of the ethical question as it may appear to Christian faith. To this end, the present chapter will analyze a few of the alternative ways in which the ethical problem has been formulated, and, more particularly, will examine the ruling presuppositions which guide the answers offered. The following chapter will attempt to lay out in as full as manner as possible a confessional statement of the answer to the moral question as it comes to us within a Christian context.

As we survey the answers made to the ethical questions stated above, we are immediately struck by the great variety of positions which have been advanced. Follow the dictate of the categorical imperative whose imperious "ought" is legislated by the universal rational will within. Treat persons as ends, never merely as means. So speaks Kant. Seek pleasure for yourself, suggests the egoistic hedonist. You already do seek it, whether or not you recognize it, so you ought to fulfill yourself by consciously seeking it. The utilitarian less crassly advises us to determine the good by reference to the maximum happiness of the greatest number of persons— though he may admit that certain higher "pleasures" should take precedence over lower ones. Realize your ideal, rational self, freed from irrational impulse and baser desires, the ethic of self-realization suggests. Aim at the absolute values of truth, beauty, and goodness which rational intuition exposes to you, the value theorist recommends. Give up the search for unchanging values, the pragmatist and relativist scornfully cry. You are chasing a will-o'-the-wisp. Settle for practical solutions to immediate concrete problems. What works to a successful conclusion is sufficient to live by in this problem-ridden world. The Marxist affirms the good as that which promotes the classless society, the overthrow of bourgeois culture, and the victory of the revolutionary proletariat. The Christian utilitarian (Paley) chimes in with the opinion that we are to do good to others for the sake of everlasting happiness in the world to come. The Biblical legalist claims that the rules of conduct are once and for all transcribed in God's verbally inspired book, while some Christian liberals may tell us that Jesus laid down general ethical principles of love and peace and the Golden Rule, which it is desirable to follow. The logical positivist threatens to squelch this torrent of ethical admonition by coldly reminding us that all supposedly ethical propositions are either logical nonsense or reports of states of feeling without the slightest semblance of objectivity or universality. Ethics, it would appear, is nothing but a branch of logic or semantics dealing with propositions the majority of which could as well be expressed by ejaculations of disgust or pleasure.

In the face of these many attempts to deal systematically with the goals of the moral life, we have to admit that no one formulation of either the ethical question or its answer has succeeded in winning possession of the field. We seem to be no more capable today of working out a rational solution to moral issues or their substantiation than were Plato, Aristotle, the Stoics, Kant, or Butler in their days. In dismay one modern author surveys the plight of moral philosophy in these terms: "What everyone hopes for as a guide are rules by which to settle all cases applicable with ease, and in some way, to everyone alike. Instead, what we have available is a procedure calling on many and fallible qualities of mind; a procedure which yields some broad and fairly obvious answers, but which for the rest leaves us to puzzle things out for ourselves, with a margin for error and disagreement too wide for comfort."[3] It is highly unlikely that a systematic Christian ethic will be developed which will succeed when so many have already failed.[4] But, we may point out, Christian faith may not be called upon to assume the task if it takes another approach to morality than that represented by the classic formulations.

At least the confusion in ethical theory does indicate most clearly that men cannot live without entering in some fashion into the depth of the choice between right and wrong, good and evil. The high seriousness with which the moral issue has been repeatedly met shows that in spite of the difficulties, verbal, logical, or practical, there is a dimension of existence which is irreducibly significant for persons. We did not invent it; we cannot evade it. We appear to be caught in a world where morality is inescapable, but where, at the same time, we cannot provide universally acceptable answers to the issues raised by it. Speculative answers seem to end in confused wrangling, banalities, or subservience to cultural forces.

Two preliminary observations may help us establish our relation to this confused scene. Can it be, first of all, that the typical expositions of the ethical question have been stated in the light of a false or incomplete perspective? If an ethical position initiates its inquiry with the firm conviction that morality deals only with intrahuman relations, and that any connection with a divine nature destroys its autonomy, then obviously the nature of deity is completely irrelevant to the conclusion[5]—even if occasionally it be tacked on as a sop to the religious mind. If God is not taken seriously from the outset, in either the formulation of the ethical question or the proposed answer, then it is highly unlikely that He can be consistently and meaningfully introduced at the final stage of ethical speculation. The basic situation of man before God, so crucial for a Christian understanding of moral theory and action, will in such a case be waved aside as irrelevant. But this wider context of the human situation cannot be so cavalierly treated, I believe, without falsifying both the moral question and any proposed answers to it. Morality, as I shall suggest, transcends itself both by virtue of its inherent religious presuppositions and by its tendency to pass over into the religious realm when moral failure, guilt, forgiveness, and renewed motivation are in question—with these experiences ethical systems have been distressingly reluctant to deal. It may also become clear that any ethical system which aspires to be taken seriously as a working framework for human behavior must come at last to terms with the character of ultimate reality—even if it tries its best to hide the fact that with certain ultimate perspectives it would be completely unintelligible, not to say hopelessly unworkable.

In the second place, we may observe that the clash of rival ethical systems derives less from lack of logical acumen and consistency or insincerity than from divergence in initial presuppositions. The stage is set for conflicting answers because initial decisions have been made, consciously or unconsciously, about what is of ultimate and absolute worth for human beings. Careful study of the ethical positions previously mentioned reveals that at some point logically prior to the systems themselves some values have been embraced as self-evidently "good" or "right." These value presuppositions are not established as universally cogent by the arguments advanced in the ethical systems themselves; they are matters of direct self-validating intuitions. For example, either one immediately recognizes self-fulfillment, pleasure, happiness, duty, truth, honesty, or the inherent worth of rational personality as supremely worthful, or else the systems built upon these concepts immediately lose their persuasive power. They do not convince, as it were, an "outsider." For this reason, no ethical system possesses the degree of autonomy or universality which its proponents usually affirm for it. The prior orientation of the moral philosopher has influenced both the posing of the ethical question and the proposed answer to it. H. R. Niebuhr observes that the supreme ethical question is always "In what does man trust?" "Moral reasoning," he concludes, "always builds on the explicit or implicit answer given to this prior question."[6] It is not remarkable, therefore, that moral philosophers who do not pay attention to the question of their own faith commitments should develop systems which so often contradict the proposals of others. Neither is it strange that their peculiar moral conclusions should be singularly unconvincing to their rivals.

It would appear that the clue to the difficulties in which moral philosophy finds itself lies less in the content of the developed systems than in the attitudes and assumptions with which the systematic ethicist goes about his task. The yearning for autonomy for morality and ethical thought and the failure to take seriously the personal commitment which one has are factors outside the field of ethics proper, yet they appear to be of decisive importance in understanding the character of ethical systems. Presuppositions, as always, become the central factors to be examined. So without entering into a detailed study of the various ethical positions which have held the center of the stage, we may seek out those assumptions which form the unquestioned structure of ethical thought as we have known it in the Western world.

The principal presupposition which appears to control ethical speculation is that of universality. The moralist, though he may deal with problems one by one, has before him the idea of the universal system. He aims at or holds to the standards of consistency and breadth of coverage. All cases of ethical dubiety, in principle, should fall within the scope of his treatment. And finally, a system should be developed which has universal relevance and internal logical consistency. To accomplish these desired aims, the moralist either aspires to or supposes he has achieved the posture of the universal spectator of moral phenomena. His use of reason is accordingly postulated on this viewpoint. He thinks as a spectator; he thinks as one committed to universality. Furthermore, he must assume that a system, realized or projected, possesses the quality of absoluteness. If and when universality is achieved, it brings with it the dimension of inescapable authority. Universality, it is supposed, is the opposite side of the coin of absoluteness. Thus even the ethical relativist must claim for his position universal and absolute validity for all inquiring, straight-thinking minds. A philosophical moralist who claims less would brand himself as either frivolous or irrational.

Let us see how the presupposition of universality may work itself out. Behind every ethical system there stands the thinker, a particular, finite human being who presumably is setting out to construct the universal system. What is his position in respect to morals? Where shall he begin? Although he is a reflective person, he cannot commence his work with reflection. He must as a responsible thinker begin somewhere to cut into the mass of ethical data he has before him, but he cannot accomplish this seemingly simple job without contradicting the universality of the system he proposes to himself. He cannot reflect himself into his systematic inquiry without first making a choice, consciously or unconsciously, of the particular, by which he grasps his material at some definite point. Perhaps some particular type of ethical action or value excites his attention (pleasure, duty, self-realization); perhaps, though it is doubtful, he selects some fragment of the data merely to have a starting point for reflection. One thing he is unable to do—to treat the whole mass of ethical data as though he himself were a universal or all-comprehending mind; he must begin with a resolve which stands outside the universality of whatever system he develops. He must act and think in the particular or singular, at least in this respect.[7]

Granted this initial methodological necessity, the moralist in his quest for universality may slip into another assumption. If he seriously aims at a system of universal scope, he must translate himself, albeit surreptitiously, into the role of the universal spectator of moral realities. Strictly speaking, he must identify himself from the outset with humanity at large to be able to think and legislate for humanity. C. A. Bennett has described the moral man, whom we can take as our hypothetical philosopher, as "the man of principle, the impartial man. He surveys the issues of conduct not merely through his own eyes, but through the eyes of all humanity."[8] Certainly not all moral philosophers would so self-consciously adopt the pose of the universal spectator, but their intent and the demands of the universal require nothing less of them.

Unfortunately, not only the personal commitments of the philosophers but the cultural assumptions of the period in which he works have a way of peeking through the system. Aristotle sees the good or happy society as one which bears a suspicious likeness to idealized Greek culture, in which even human slavery has a place. Certain virtues, such as generosity, fall outside the orbit of a poor man's "good life," since only a person of means and leisure can fulfill them. Even the deity of Aristotle, which thinks about thinking, has an uncomfortable resemblance to the philosopher's status as a thinker who takes intrinsic pleasure in thinking. Kant's magnificent attempt to understand the universal right in terms of rational will and freedom is flecked with traces of the Age of Revolution in which he lived; behind his reaction against a morality of sentiment can be descried the enthusiastic pietism which he rejected.[9] His notion of deity as hidden in the impenetrable reaches of the noumenal, is likewise less the deliverance of "pure reason" than the outworking of the notion of God's transcendence handed down from medieval theology. Hegel's apotheosis of the Prussian state as the ideal political order is but the most palpable evidence of the failure of the universally minded spectator. For better or worse there seem to be no universal men to do universal thinking, to construct universal systems; there are only finite men with more or less comprehensive perspectives on human existence. Those who essay to be moral philosophers in general dissolve into particular participants rather than effectively maintaining their postures as universal spectators of the shifting relativities of experience.

Allegiance to the notion of universality may go further in its effects. Even as the moralist may attempt to lose himself in lofty universal perspectives of the good or right, he may also fashion his system for everybody—the anonymous, faceless nobody in particular. To be of universal application, the system must be constructed with this hypothetical entity in mind, though the euphemism of "all rational men" or "all right thinking" may be substituted for Mr. Everybody. The most concrete way in which this drive for universal applicability and scope shows itself is in the confident expectation that the good or right may be stated as a principle, rule, maxim, or law, which is, or at least ought to be, universally accepted by "right-thinking people." The morally good life, by common consent, is one lived by principle, not by fluctuating sentiment. To this conclusion even the consistent hedonist must come. "You ought always to seek pleasure." "You ought always to seek happiness." "You ought always to treat persons as ends, never as means only." "You ought always to solve moral problems by the scientific method." Such in their boldest terms are the universal rules laid down in typical ethical systems. In the formulation of these maxims, however, the thinker moves increasingly away from any conscious relation to concrete, personal, or social choices. He deals with the reified vitalities of human experience and abstract cases, devoid of cultural and psychological circumstances. In fact, as morality turns more and more to the development of rules and principles, it seems always to be at one step removed from any moral behavior. Empathetic relation to the specific seems to mar the ideal universality of the system. Detachment, neutrality, and objectivity are the necessary attitudes for ethical reflection in its search for the universal. The dynamic must be made static, and this can be accomplished only by resolute conceptualization.

So universalism calls to its aid the one instrument which it is presumed can make universal judgments, the human reason. Reason in its critical phase can clear up the inconsistencies of moral thinking. It draws attention to certain partial goals with which we have become overconcerned. It can point up the wretched differences which constantly show up between our professions of ethical ideals and our moral conduct. Its greatest value is that it can repeatedly correct itself—provided, of course, there is the "good will" to do so! Without reason in its critical form, the ethical quest goes into bankruptcy from the beginning. At last every pattern of ethical reflection, whether it be avowedly rationalistic or empirical, must come to the bar of autonomous reason to receive its accolade of verification. They must be "reasonable" or "logical" systems or they are worthless. If the moral good or right can be and ought to be formulated as principles, then reason naturally must be called upon both to fashion and to criticize these principles. However, criticism is not enough for the ethicist; reason must proceed to its synthesizing phase. Reason, or rather the thinker, intent upon realizing universality, attempts to draw into a comprehensive unity the multiplicity of value-claims and to render in consistent, orderly form an account of the total structure of moral experience. In fact, moral reasoning finds one of its principal methods of verification in the system. Logical coherence is one of the supreme tests of universal validity.

In speaking critically of this aspect of the search for universality, I am not entering into the centuries-old quarrel between faith and reason as methods of knowing God or one's moral responsibilities. It has been my steady purpose to refuse to do battle on behalf of faith as an alternative or superior way of knowledge, precisely because even to set up a conflict of this type is to beg the question as to whether faith as I conceive it provides knowledge.[10] Whenever the lines between faith and reason are drawn as a debate about a theory of knowledge, faith plays false to itself by surrendering at the outset its uniqueness. Some years ago P. H. Waddell saw the danger of this procedure. "So long as Christian theology is guided . . . by the syllogisms of the logical understanding, it has first to cast all the truths it wishes to express into an argumentative form, which exhausts their spirituality before they find expression."[11] Such a treatment of faith caricatures the meaning of faith as a mode of existence, as developed in these pages.

Christian faith aims neither at rationalism, irrationalism, nor even fideism, for that matter. It declines to accept the traditional dilemma of either autonomous reason or obscurantism. It accepts the inevitability of reason's use, as it does all gifts from the divine hand, but refuses to absolutize it because it is, after all, set within the framework of finite and sinful men. Reason is not a master, unbridled in authority; it is prone to follow the dispositions of the human self in which it dwells. Yet reason itself is not sinful, darkened in such a way as to be of no use in ethics or the religious life. Man, not some one of his faculties, is the sinner. In fact, reason must be sufficiently trustworthy, in our reading of the Christian faith, to be capable of reliably informing us that we are sinners! Or, as Dr. John Baillie has argued: "I would affirm that a totally corrupt being would be as incapable of sin as would a totally illogical being of fallacious argument."[12]

Both by finitude and by sin reason may be and often is led aside. If it does not serve God—nor faith—it serves the interests of the self or culture. It defends its authenticity not simply by self-scrutiny or by extended argumentation, or, as Karl Jaspers points out, by our knowledge of it—all of which presupposes the very validity which reason aims to establish logically—but by passing into practice "in the sciences, in everyday life, and intellectual works that penetrate more deeply into the truth than the sciences are able to do."[13] By its passage into the state of existence, mindful of its obedience to its donor and ultimate goal, it finds its true freedom.

When reason is depended upon as the agent of universality, it may indeed give a wider view of ethical realities, but it does not follow that reason brings about a wider commitment or concern of the self. Neither, for that matter, does its conviction of our ethical inconsistencies enable us as existing selves to achieve that integrity and consistency which we lack. "Consistency," as Reinhold Niebuhr maintains, "is the achievement of the self rather than of its reason, because there is no power in reason as such to compel consistency, though it may have the power to detect inconsistency in the pursuit of goals."[14]

The lure of the universal and absolute draws the moralist into an exciting and yet ultimately frustrating chase. Reason feeds upon the category of the "possible," and can, as it were, endlessly spin out of itself possibilities in its vain quest for a universal framework which will interpret all instances of choice and action. But it runs itself to exhaustion because the dynamic elements of the thinker's own existence and those of humanity at large repeatedly slip through the net of the possible. The partial, the unique, and the particular defy the universal, while the actual, the concrete, and the nonrational make the possible look irrelevant. The tidiness of the moralist's mind is consistently outraged by the nasty habit which these alternatives possess of reducing his system to a shambles of miscellaneous pronouncements and *ad hoc* hypotheses. The ethical thinker can easily withstand intellectual attacks on his position; these take place within the framework of reason. But when choice, action, and motivation are in question, he finds himself unprepared, by the dictates of reason operating on a universalistic outlook, to deal with them. They are interlopers from another realm. The call to choice and action pulls one out of the sphere of the possible into the concrete.

Two principal problems plague the moralist. The first is the perplexity which surrounds the matter of motivation. Theoretically the vision or insight into the good or right should so immediately commend itself to men that forthwith they act and judge in the light of it—barring physical impossibility. Knowledge of the good or right should automatically produce the desire for the good or right and the consequence of moral action. But a step or two are missing. Some people stubbornly see the good or right yet fail in desiring or achieving it. The motivation for choice has not been born. This unfortunate state of affairs is to be explained along rationalistic lines, by the supposition that the delinquent person has not really understood or known the good or right. If he had, he would act accordingly.[15] All that remains is to enlighten his ignorance by further instruction and argument. Yet no argument or intellectual enlightenment helps one over the divide between the possible and the act of will by which this possible is made concrete. If the will is lacking, the teachings and maxims fall on deaf ears. The person, strictly speaking, is not free to desire or will the good. The "ought" has neither generated nor brought to expression the "is" of freedom. It has only confirmed the impossibility of freedom in effective action.

This problem is made no easier of solution when it is recognized that not only a universal but an absolute claim has been entered against the self. As we have seen, ethical systems derive their appearance of vitality from the close connection between absoluteness and universality. This is most clearly seen in Kant, but virtually every ethical formulation presupposes the union. But this assumption is one of the most questionable elements in any ethical system. We may repeatedly be told we "ought" absolutely to will the universal good, but how this "ought" becomes genuinely authoritative for me is left hanging. If I autonomously legislate it for myself, why should I obey it? What authority do I have over myself? How does the fact that I have a reason which legislates universally derive its authority? From a universal reason? But that is to take

away its authority *for me* and deposit it in the universal. If it comes
to me from society, its voice turns out to be the sum of social ex-
pediency masquerading as universal reason, and forthwith sheds
its majestic absoluteness. Do the universal and absolute genuinely
form one ethical unit, or are they distinguishable and separable in
act if not in thought?

I may find myself in a situation where I am unable rationally
to will my projected action as a universal for others, even in an
identical situation—if there ever were such! Yet, standing in this
crisis of choice and action, I may feel myself called absolutely to
carry out a certain course. The absoluteness of the demand may be
in no intelligible relation to that which the anonymous "every man"
ought to do, because I only stand here and now in that immediate
situation with this particular responsibility to act. I cannot determine
the correctness of my proposed action by universalizing it in my
imagination—my imagination being limited by both sin and finitude. I must face, instead, the possibility of error and guilt for and by
myself. The absoluteness of the demand is then incommensurate
with the presupposition of universalism.

Of course, what we have been exploring above is the age-old
theme of rational principle versus concrete choice and action. And
as we do so, it becomes clearer that choice and action, or personal
existence, is a serious check to all systematic ethical speculation which
presupposes universality and absoluteness.

We find in those systems of ethics which seek the rationally
universal good two movements of thought. In one phase the thinker
moves "upward" and away from social customs, the individual
peculiarities of selves and cultures, in order to distill the quint-
essence of the ethical good or right. The particularities of the immediate are accordingly submerged or lost sight of as one ascends
to the realm of rational principles which, if and when it is achieved,
combines universal scope and validity with absoluteness of authority.
If someone suggests that a high price has been paid for this ascent
in the loss of relevance to concrete choices and action, it may be
replied that the task of the ethicist is not that of giving guidance
or bridging the gap between the universal and the particular. We
have simply failed to understand the moralists' purpose, which is that
of giving a coherent account of moral phenomena, and the derivation of universal norms. Whether or not they are applied is quite
another matter. The ethical philosopher looks to the lines along

which solutions to moral dilemmas may be seen, or he criticizes the reasoning which has led to proposed solutions. This viewpoint, however, in sum admits the charge of irrelevance of ethical speculation to life choices, but claims that such was never its serious purpose. The ethicist is serious—of that we have no right to complain; unfortunately, he is often more serious about thinking than about morality itself. He makes clear to us that he is engaged in "pure" ethics, and in this role he must be left while the rest of humanity goes on as best it may.[16] On the other hand, the charge of irrelevance may be met by the type of answer which would be consistent with Kantian ethics. The moral philospher has shown men what they ought to do; he has demonstrated the rational grounds of the "ought" and its content. What remains is what always remains to be done where principle and existence meet: apply the rule, exercise and obey the "ought." No further can any ethical system go in coming to grips with choice and action.

Yet a third type of answer is sometimes offered to the charge of irrelevance. The sensitive moralist, perhaps aware of the hollowness of his universal principles, begins to fill in the gap between the universal and moral behavior by a "downward" movement of thought which will make specific the applicability of the universal. As though appalled and conscience-stricken at the gulf between the concrete and the universal which he has dug, the moralist may begin to spell out with care the bridging steps by which one may return from the universal to the specifics of moral action. He feels he must descend, by easy steps of decompression, to life. When this happens, legalism has set in. The noble, inspiring horizons which the search for the universal opened to us begin to be clouded over by moralism, which in aiming at the specific applicability of the universal, confines and narrows the human spirit in its freedom. We are driven by the austere injunctions of the legalist into what Bonhoeffer called "trite and jejune moralization and a pedantic regimentation of the whole of life."[17] Thus, for example, the Plato of the Republic loses caste in the petty legislation of the *Laws* as he attempts to come to grips with the specifics of a real "ideal" state!

It is not the philosophical moralists who most commonly ward off the charge of irrelevance by legalism. Usually legalism has arisen within religious outlooks where theologians have adopted the function and attitudes of the moral philosopher. In Judaism and Christianity, when the will of God has been construed as law, legalism is not far off. Still operating with the ideal of universality, the religious casuist moves from the idea of God's law to God's laws, and their application to daily conduct. The entire transition, from the standpoint of Christian faith, is a movement away from the absoluteness of God's demand, met in the unique situation, to the rules spun out from an original law to meet specific cases.

Legalism does not originate with designing lawyers, priests, and theologians who wish to burden men with regulations. Rather it arises out of a solicitude that the will of God be made as clear as possible, that men shall be helped to apply the appropriate rule to the problem in question, and, above all, that men may escape guiltless from moral perplexity. In laying out the divisions and subdivisions of divine law, legalism answers the charge of irrelevance by relieving men, so far as possible, from the agony of doubt, ignorance, and consequent guilt. It proposes to reduce ethical ambiguity to the vanishing point by making crystal clear the nature of the "right" choice. It brings the disheveled scene of moral confusion into order by showing that increasingly specific rules may be derived rationally from the original universal law of God. It shows its practical intent by dealing with cases of conscience as variations upon some broader ethical principles which in turn are referred to the authority of God himself. It aims to cover life, to become virtually coexistent with it, so as to leave no case in doubt or outside its sweep of authority. But to accomplish this ideal goal, legalism sets about the never-ending proliferation of regulations and duties. Its fixed ideas of relevance, universality, and guiltlessness never permit it to halt until these ends have been achieved—which is never! Then there follows the law expert, for only one versed in the intricacies of ethical principles and conversant with the wide range of typical cases can hope to formulate detailed regulations or decide which regulation takes precedence over another in practice. Moral choice increasingly becomes the task of the professional, and the "common man," for whom the apparatus of legalism has been constructed, finds his choice restricted to that between one expert and another. Morality by proxy becomes the established mode; the law, the laws, and the expert stand resolutely between the individual and his own responsibility as a moral being.

However, the ultimate sanction of legalism lies less in its claim to solicitude for man's ethical guidance than in its appeal to the universality and absoluteness of the divine law. As God reigns universally and absolutely, so must his law partake of universality and absoluteness. Similarly, though this is seldom worked out to its fullest extent, all deductions of subsidiary regulations of the law take on the authority of the divine. To break even the least of these is a flagrant attack upon the authority of God. So legalism rests logically upon the strongest sanction of all, and defies all efforts, short of revolution by atheism or faith, to break its hold upon the minds and spirits of men.

When legalism reaches this extreme, its effect upon human existence is depressing and stultifying. Men learn that the accumulation of duties, each bearing the weight of the divine, smothers them with regulations which they have not the slightest chance of fulfilling short of eternity. They are guilt-ridden because, to be loyal to the letter of the law, they must obey, yet they cannot or will not. They must choose certain laws to be of superior value to others, thereby breaking the assumption of the universality and absoluteness of the whole apparatus. Or they may doggedly work at righteousness piecemeal, hoping against hope that sometime, somehow, the moral life will be rounded out. Yet for every rule fulfilled, another goes unfulfilled, and the tedious business must begin afresh until all power and interest is spent. At the same time, when life is lived under legalism, one must keep alert to the progress one is making, and this is most often done by comparing oneself with others. Of this plight the classic scriptural illustration is the story of the Pharisee and the publican, going up to the temple to pray. The Pharisee's estimate of his religious and moral accomplishment is made on the basis of a "horizontal" comparison with other men. The publican sees himself before the righteousness of God, the "vertical," and his life is made anew in repentance and by mercy.

If legalism is accepted as the characteristic form of systematic ethics, theological or philosophical, it brings in its train just such defensiveness, conservatism, and presumed guiltlessness as the story depicts. It seeks to preserve status; it looks back to past achievement; it takes no chances or proposes no revolutions. It seeks above all, as do all ethical systems at root, to bring the person through blameless. It produces moral prigs and ethically insensitive persons by its overemphasis upon a morality of doing the right thing by conscious forethought. Yet great moral character seldom comes by focusing attention upon itself, but, as in the case of happiness, is a by-product of a life lived in total personal responsibility. Legalism sparks men to no fresh attacks upon social injustice. It gives no place to that reckless largeness of sympathy which dares storm heaven and give life away for that which will outlast it. It brings to heel spontaneous acts of kindness and generosity, which might make fools of us, and settles for what one author has called "pigeon-hearted rectitude." The judgment upon morality functioning in legalistic form has been pronounced by Bennett: "The attempt to live exclusively in the light of the strenuously comparative estimate of one's value ends by producing a society whose marks are timidity, conventionality and uniformity. For the individual it means at worst the suffocation of originality, at best a perpetual uneasiness."[18]

For Christian faith, the error of legalism lies not only in what it does to human life but in what it implies about God. Legalism operates upon the implicit belief that God is not the living God of Jesus Christ, but One who as a lawgiver has once and for all stated all that He has to say on religious and moral behavior. Legalism supposes that it has harnessed the power and authority of the sovereign God, and thereby has disposed of His freedom, upon which at last man's true freedom is grounded. God has no further light to break forth; He has ceased to exist in man's present, to all intents and purposes, and man is left to live on the inert scraps of revelation long past. Gone is the moment-to-moment existence which faith knows before God; gone is the God-man polarity as the tension between them is dissolved into a steadily increasing mass of legal detail. And the result, as Paul and many others have found, is despair, exhaustion, and hopelessness. Legalism never can deliver what it promises—relevance, universality, and absoluteness of ethical direction and guiltlessness.

Now we seem to have swept away all possibility of ethical guidance. We have left men adrift on the broad sea of ethical anarchy and indifferentism. And, in a sense, that is where man is without faith. It is only as he sees how desperate his situation is that he can come to himself and come upon morality as a new possibility for the expression of his existence. But this is certainly not the end of the matter. The law and the sense of "ought" which we find in all men does have its setting within a faith-ethic. God has not left Himself without witness in humanity. We do not deny law and the sense of "ought" a part in the Christian life, though we do deny legalism as a proper derivation from them.

Law and moral obligation are not strictly correlated. Wherever the moral law confronts man in its deepest sense, it affirms or pre-supposes the ought, but it does not follow that every instance of moral obligation is also an evidence of law. There must ever remain the concrete personal demand (not law) of God, which is absolute, yet not universal. The ought, therefore, is a more primary category than that of law. In agreement with much of the serious ethical thought of moral philosophy, Christian faith holds that moral obligation is an abiding irreducible and irreplaceable constituent of man's nature. It refuses to identify it with liking or desiring or a product of "socialization." In fact, socialization presupposes the ought, though the ought finds its content in its dialogue with men and God. Neither does faith see the ought as a kind of autonomous, self-sufficient power in man, for it fulfills itself in the "ought to do" or "ought to be," thereby revealing its fundamental relational character. Furthermore, the ought remains irreducible, not because it shows us to be inescapably moral persons, but because it estab-lishes us in sin. It is the constant reminder of the enormous divorce-ment between ourselves and the love of God seen in Jesus Christ.

Thus when the law or the demand of God speaks to us with a "you ought," we cannot overlook lightly what it is fundamentally saying. In these instances, the ought is not God's voice of recon-ciliation and love primarily; it is that which singles us out as being responsible to choose and act, here and now, even when we do not want to do so. We may wince, struggle, or even attempt to explain away this ought, but it ruthlessly pins us to this situation with immediacy and particularity. It convicts us not only for some particular act undone in the past, or as yet unaccomplished in the future, but for being in the condition we are, estranged from our-selves, our fellow men, and God.

Every moral ought throws into bold relief some phase of our ex-istence, for each reminds us that what we now are is set at a distance from that which we see as commanded as our duty. The ought is the symbol of this gap or estrangement in our personal existence, where desire and obligation fall apart. The implication to be drawn from the presence of the ought in man is not, as Kant so quickly concluded, freedom without which we could not be held responsible. Rather the ought implies the lack of freedom which frustrates the unification of desire and obligation. It signifies the "I will not" or "I cannot." For at least the opening moments of any ethical struggle, we are aware that we are judged, in this very struggle, by the fact that desire and will do not accord, or self and others conflict. We are the kind of persons who need an ought to stir us to action; we do not spontaneously generate virtue—and when we are sensitively honest with ourselves, we know it. But more than that, we recognize that this disrupted state of existence in which we find ourselves is not a momentary or transient condition but the mode of existence in which we continue to live —set at a distance from ourselves, others, and God. From the standpoint of Christian faith, this is the judgment under which we live; it is the weight from which we would be freed.

Yet we look at the ought not simply as the evidence of judgment. Regarding it in the broader light of our theocentric position, we see it also as an act of mercy opening to us the possibility of growth and transformation. It remains within the Christian life as the effectual reminder, not only of our fragmented and unfulfilled being, but of the love of One who cares enough to judge us and lure us toward reconciliation with Himself, others, and ourselves.

The moral imperative thus bears a double aspect as the mark of judgment and the mark of moral possibility. The ought, in the latter form, comes before us as the sign of something of ourselves from which we have turned away. It recalls us to an integrity of existence of which we have all the time had some intimation. Thus it represents not some alien element thrust into the midst of our lives from the outside, as it were, by the sheer power of God. It is part of ourselves which God destined us to be, now come back to demand our choice of it. "The law given by God," as Tillich puts it, "is man's essential nature, put against him as law. If man were not estranged from himself, if his essential nature were not distorted in his actual existence, no law would stand against him. The law is not strange to man. . . . It represents his true nature from which he is estranged. Every valid ethical commandment is an expression of man's essential relation to himself, to others, and to the universe. This alone makes it obligatory and its denial self-destructive. This alone accounts for the unconditional form of the moral imperative, however questionable and conditioned the contents may be."[19]

The sense of law which presupposes the ought is incorporated in the life of Christian faith because the fulfillment, no less than the judgment, is an integral part of our existence as Christians. With Paul we may regard the moral law as a "pedagogue," which leads and guides toward the ultimate relation with God, but which never enters into it with us. It does not as sheer command produce love of our neighbor or God, but it may provide the structure of human life within which love and reconciliation may flourish. In fact, it makes it necessary that they do so by its limitations and failure to achieve the final good in legislative terms. Law makes possible the more or less orderly organization of our common life by compromising, suppressing, and controlling our incipient anarchies and irresponsibilities. Because men are not equal in personal endowments, in their potential contributions to society, or in ethical discrimination, the law, operating on the principle of justice, distributes the power of societies into those arrangements which afford the maximum equality of opportunity consistent with the order of a society.[20] Against the potential disorder and injustice of human life, law serves as a bulwark and, by its continuity and conservatism, preserves the hard-won gains from the welter of individual and social egoisms. Our capacity for law, furthermore, is the foundation for growth and education in ethical discrimination and responsibility. Moral conscience is not a ready-made affair; it is a capacity which may be trained. Without the operation of reason in both its critical and its synthetic phases, such training would be impossible. Without man's initial moral sensitivity, which conscience affords, reason would be operating in a vacuum. Out of the components of social experience, reason, and conscience, man fashions law. And this law in turn forms the transient but necessary framework of guidance for the morally developing self. Law, therefore, is a precondition of moral growth as well as a product thereof. Our capacity for law, by wrestling with the tough problems of social existence, continuously establishes norms of behavior in the light of which ethical development may occur, sometimes even going beyond the level of moral opinion at a given time.[21] Without this guidance, backed by public opinion, power, and the sense of the ought, society would be impossible. Law is the "pedagogue" of human life, though its dictates, for Christian faith, can never be taken as final. So long as sin and finitude, with their consequent shortcomings in social imagination, insight, and responsibility, remain, law also remains as the foundation, but not the summit, of human existence. As Christ is the end of the law, faith refuses to state the supreme good in terms of laws, duties, or values. Beyond these is the culminating event of existence in faith.

Universality and absoluteness, the presupposition and goal of moral philosophy, coincide in no human formulation, but only in God Himself. No law or duty, no value, no principle of action, however clearly and fully expounded, encompasses and expresses divine love.[22] It cannot be legislated because ultimately it is itself the precondition of human existence. It can only be responded to in choice and action in whatever measure of freedom faith opens to us. Faith sees the law pointed toward this love; it sees the law judged by it, but it does not believe that such love can ever be brought within the structure of law, even at the highest point of its development.

It in no way discredits the role of law and moral obligation to point out that an ethic which accepts the supremacy of these two foci of moral development falls afoul of at least two problems. These are the problems of motivation, to which I have alluded, and the experience of moral failure. It is not my purpose to argue that Christian faith resolves these issues in any final fashion, but it is important to show the inadequacy of any ethic which does not take seriously these problems and to suggest that they do bring us to the threshold of the domain of faith.

Emil Brunner has charged that natural morality and ethics "seeks exclusively to answer the question 'What ought I to do?' It deals only with conduct, not with the person who acts."[23] Accordingly, it would appear, ethics and law need not be concerned about the motivations out of which a person acts. So long, for example, as I drive on the correct side of the road, thereby contributing to the safety of my fellow human beings, ethics and law care nothing as to whether I do so out of grudging conformity to law, habit, or a full sense of responsibility for human life. Presumably, the act alone is of significance. In this and kindred senses Brunner is undoubtedly right. However, as in the case of murder, the judge and jury, here representing a natural ethics, do take into consideration the motivations of the suspect in weighing his guilt, or in passing sentence upon him if he is found guilty. It is not only the act, but the total attendant conditions, inclusive of personal motivation, which must be taken into consideration so far as these may be determined. In this respect, Brunner has overstated his case. Yet so far as representative ethical theory is concerned, more often than not the act, not the motive, is held to be alone subject to ethical judgment. As Sir David Ross has argued, we cannot control our motives; they are simply what they are at a given time; therefore we are under obligation only to do a certain act and to consider only the act as a fit subject of ethical judgment.[24] This position, as H. D. Lewis has pointed out in his *Morals and Revelation,* is not beyond serious criticism by moral philosophers.

Our question, however, is primarily concerned, not with the proper subjects of ethical judgments by others, but with the conditions of any act which may fall under the judgment of others. Protestant theology has been firm in holding that the ethical unit is not only the overt act but the person as such, and though this position involves great difficulties, it remains from any existential perspective the most profitable starting point for ethical theory. The self is the fount of moral action, and any arbitrary or methodological device which separates the agent from the act sunders the original complex into artificial parts which may be easier to deal with rationally but in their separation change the problem with which we are basically concerned.

That problem is one of empowering the self to do what he thinks is right, good, or of supreme value. It is notoriously true that the sense of ought or the idea of law does not by its presence summon up the will or desire to fulfill it. It is equally true that ethical philosophy and theology have been singularly reluctant to touch this thorny issue. Perhaps Kant came closest to doing so, and even he had to break over into the religious realm. He found himself faced with the insoluble problem of "radical evil in human nature" confronting the categorical imperative, and could discover no way out but to resort to what Jesus, Augustine, and the Reformers had maintained, i.e., a change of heart. Let Kant speak for himself:

But that a man should become not merely a legally but morally good (God-pleasing) man, that is, virtuous in his intelligible character . . . a man who, when he recognizes a thing as his duty, needs no other spring than this conception of duty itself; this is not effected by gradual reform . . . but requires a revolution in the mind . . . and he can only become a new man by a kind of new birth, as it were a new creation and a change of heart. . . .
Hence it follows that the moral culture of man must begin, not with improvement of morals, but with a transformation of the mind and the foundation of a character, although men usually proceed other-

wise, and contend against vices singly, leaving the general root of them untouched.[25]

If it be true that the fullest ethical fulfillment demands my self, yet my self in its deepest motivations rebels against duty or the achievement of the higher values, what alternatives can be proposed by which to consummate this unity of the self with the ought? I cannot act simply out of fear of evil consequences or prudential self-interest without thereby revealing to myself my plight. The division between the ought and desire is only made the sharper. If I warn myself that I will be guilty of rational inconsistency if I do not perform what I ought to or fail to accomplish what the law or higher self commands, I am met by the comment that "Man cannot live his life with no better guide than that afforded by the law of non-contradiction."[26] Nor am I better off if I attempt by strenuous imagination to see value where none exists for me at present.[27] The reiteration of the ought simply does not draw me into wholehearted relation to the good—as the fulfillment of my being—though I may carry out what I think I ought to do, and for this possibility humanity may well be thankful.

There may be different ways to overcome this failure of motivation, but in terms of Christian faith there seems to be no way out but the "expulsive power of a new affection" which comes by virtue of a new relation with God, man, and the self. Conversion, nothing else, as Kant saw it, lies at the root of the matter, and thus morality must at last come to terms with faith.

This is the truth embedded in Augustine's profound summary of the relation of law to grace. "For neither is the law fulfilled except by free will; but by the law is the knowledge of sin, by faith, the acquisition of grace against sin, by grace the healing of the soul from the disease of sin, by the health of the soul freedom of will, by free will, the love of righteousness, by love of righteousness, the accomplishment of the law."[28] Which is to say that where the ought and the law fail to engender the required motivation, the orientation of the self to its divine ground enables us by love to will and accomplish what law and virtue demand of us. The outcome of conversion, understood in this context, is not moral anarchism or the repudiation of natural ethics but the fulfillment of the latter and the structuring of moral responsibility in respect to the former. Thus we see Augustine converting, as it were, the virtues of Aristotle in the light of the love of God which he held to be the supreme virtue. Temperance, he wrote, "is love giving itself entirely to that which is loved; fortitude is love readily bearing all things for the sake of the loved object; justice is love serving only the loved object, and therefore ruling rightly; prudence is love distinguishing with sagacity between what hinders it and what helps it."[29]

The question of adequate motivation is closely bound to the altogether too familiar experience of moral failure. And again traditional forms of ethical theory are embarrassed by their inability to cope with the problem within the limits of their rationalistic systems. The most the moralist can offer is the advice to think again, and to try again, until all energy is spent. With the accumulating guilt and frustration which repeated moral failure brings, ethics has little or nothing to do. "Moral philosophers," one of their number comments, "do not seem to have had a great deal to say about guilt. . . . In recent ethics especially it has suffered much neglect."[30] Failure is apparently not a subject for proper ethical speculation, yet at no other point, perhaps, does human life reveal its serious poignancy so vividly. The word which sticks in the throat of moral philosophy is forgiveness or pardon.

Dr. E. P. Dickie says, "The system has nothing to offer to the man who fails to keep faith with the demands of duty. It cannot speak the word 'pardon.' Forgiveness is not 'ethical,' but a breach of the ethical, since strict morality demands justice, not pardon."[31] Reason must see the balances of life as even; it cannot discover a "reason" for forgiveness which would upset the balance of act and punishment. Nor can the self embroiled in guilt pronounce pardon for itself, because it would seem unworthy of its dignity to refuse the burden which it has itself contracted. Yet there is nothing so earnestly sought, for forgiveness means freedom and the new beginning with fresh energy.

Once more we confront a juncture where morality, if not ethical theory, passes over into the realm of religious faith. What no system or person, even ourselves, can do is accomplished in that act whereby we are brought in faith to accept ourselves from the hand of a forgiving God. Whereas ethics, strictly conceived, never saves from guilt and despair, but only drives us the harder toward both, even while it promises guiltlessness, faith sets us within the orbit of His forgiving love in such a way that we are no longer worn out by the round of stale effort or the depressing weight of defensiveness. If God accepts us, just as we are, not having earned His regard by superior moral achievement, then are we indeed free yet responsible as recipients of His mercy. The everlasting scowling grimness of the moral athlete is wiped out along with the surrender to cynicism or lighthearted amorality of the irresponsible. Behind every systematic ethic there lurks a yearning for redemption from ignorance and wrongdoing and a hope for personal fulfillment. Yet this is a redemption which ethics, in terms of its own presuppositions, is powerless to achieve. The way of Christian faith, by its illumination of the predicament of man and the opening of possibilities for a "new being," offers from our perspective a more realistic and promising hope than any alternative, though it by no means follows that this is the only perspective within which the moral life of man may be thought or lived.

It has been repeatedly argued that ethics and morality are independent of religious faith, and there is no point in denying that many people believe and act upon this hypothesis.[32] However, it is noteworthy, as has been suggested above, that moral action itself often presupposes and brings one to the religious realm, even when autonomy for ethics is asserted. There remains, as Tillich claims, "no answer in ethics without an explicit or implicit assertion about the nature of being."[33] Unless this were the kind of universe it is, man could neither conceive nor carry out the types of ethical possibilities he does. The nature of ultimate being does at last have bearing on ethics. If, as Shailer Mathews used to say, this is a personality-producing and -sustaining universe, then that fact has implications for the types of conduct which are both necessary and achievable. Some types of value promote human fulfillment; others, though they work for a time, fail at some crucial juncture. If we are content to leave out of consideration the impact of this wider context for ethics, we find ourselves bound either to our individual egoisms or to the immediate relativities of a particular culture, with no ground for criticism of either. Ethics turns into conformity to mores and manners, and personal authenticity is lost in conformity.

It has not been my thought to identify religious faith with ethics or morality. Religion has its category of the "holy" which cannot be equated with a high degree of moral virtue.[34] And certainly religious institutionalism has many times fallen far below or opposed the high standards of morality set forth by so-called secular morality.

However, it is our conviction that morality when properly understood arises out of fundamentally religious attitudes and therefore is never existentially autonomous, even though systematic ethical speculation may be carried on in independence of this assumption.[35] Furthermore, we conclude that morality as living experience moves man toward the crises of religious faith, though ethics may never pass over into the religious realm proper. Ethical considerations, whether understood in Kantian, eudaemonistic, value theory, or self-realization forms, do not exhaust the domain of religious faith; nor, on the contrary, does religious faith deny the unique authenticity of the ethical realm. The two are distinguishable but inseparable.[36]

We must now return to the original question of this chapter, namely, the form which the ethical question takes in the context of radical Christian faith. In the light of our analysis of the presuppositions of ethical systems and our conclusions concerning the relation of the human subject to the divine object, we find that our question has become a double-pronged one. In the first instance, the man of faith asks, "what is the God whom I have met in faith doing by way of creating or sustaining, judging, and redeeming this specific situation of ethical dubiety? What good is already being performed here and now? What is the 'isness' of God's work, seen in the form of the three-fold pattern mentioned above, in the light of which I am called upon and permitted to take action?" A. E. Taylor once pointed out that a great religion does not produce moral virtue by its commands and duties, but by "its vision of that from which we come and to which we return, . . . what it is doing and will do in and for us." For this reason, he maintained, "the regenerating moral effect of our religion on our conduct is most genuine and profound when the direct object of our attention is not the self and its task, but God."[37] Our first question then aims to understand the indicative of God's prevenient activity which lays the basis of the imperative directed to ourselves.

The second part of the ethical question is set by the circumstances which faith discovers by its preliminary query. "What am I, or what is my group, to do in response to the divine action?" Or, in more detail, "What ought and can be done here and now which, at least in some fragmentary fashion, will be both a response to the divine sustenance, judgment, and redemption and the concrete need before me?" This is to say that a man of faith, in gratitude, puts himself responsibly and sensitively at the disposal of God's will for a situation, to the limits of his reason, imagination, and courage. He does not presume to read off in advance what God wills in detail, nor does he assume that he will be miraculously safeguarded from errors of discrimination. He does not cast into an artificial wooden scheme the ambiguous particulars of a morally problematic situation. But he does hold himself alert and responsive to what God lays upon him through his neighbor's need. He has mercy, because God is merciful to him. He forgives, because he lives in forgiveness. He seeks justice, because God's judgment upon him is just. He loves, because God first loved us. Thus the indicative gives the foundation of moral attitudes and actions by arousing in us gratitude, but the specific needs determine the structure and relevant content of our acts. The truth of the moral life of Christian faith, as Donald Baillie once remarked, is that "a Christian does not live by practicing any ethic or moulding himself on any ideal, but by a faith in God which finally ascribes all good to Him."[38]

VI

Faith and Community

In this is love, not that we loved God but that he loved us. . . . We love, because he first loved us. . . . If any one says, 'I love God,' and hates his brother, he is a liar; for he who does not love his brother whom he has seen, cannot love God whom he has not seen. And this commandment we have from him, that he who loves God should love his brother also. [I John 4:10a, 19-21]

But I say to you, Love your enemies and pray for those who persecute you, so that you may be sons of your Father who is in heaven; for he makes his sun rise on the evil and on the good, and sends rain on the just and on the unjust. [Matthew 4:44-45]

For he is our peace, who has made us both one, and has broken down the dividing wall of hostility by abolishing in his flesh the law of commandments and ordinances, that he might create in himself one new man in place of the two, so making peace, and might reconcile us both to God. . . . [Ephesians 2:14-16]

For I am sure that neither death, nor life, nor angels, nor principalities, nor things present, nor things to come, nor powers, nor height, nor depth, nor anything else in all creation, will be able to separate us from the love of God in Christ Jesus our Lord. [Romans 8:38-39]

"Every ethos has its origin in a revelation, whether or not it is still aware of and obedient to it; and every revelation is revelation of human service to the goal of creation, in which service man authenticates himself."[1]

Christian faith may appropriate these words of Martin Buber, the Jewish theologian, as the broad pattern within which its ethic may move. In Christ is laid bare the judgment and love of God—this is the revelatory point, the clue to the meaning of human existence. It forms not merely a historic point of reference in our past, but is a living memory in our present. The judgment and love which has apprehended us through this man's life, teaching, death, and resurrection continues as the spirit of judgment and love which keeps step with us all the way. We are committed to Him who has acted through Christ to bring us to hold Him as the author, sustainer, and conserver of all existence. In the light of this conviction, our morality is the responsible service we undertake to the whole range of His creation, in fidelity and love. Our morality is the by-product of our faith. It is the sign of the validation of our existence in faith, but it is not directly the aim of our faith. It remains the obedient response to the revelatory acts of God which stand antecedent to our decisions and actions and which have made possible a new way of hearing and responding to His will in the present.

The Biblical witness rehearses this interplay between the objective revelatory acts of God and the transformation of man, out of which faithful obedience springs. The Ten Commandments are not the first words of God to Israel. They are prefaced by those acts of grace in which God promised Himself to Noah, to Abraham, and above all, in the establishment of the covenant, to the whole people. He first rescued them from tribal disorganization, slavery, and anarchy and on the foundation of that unmerited act goes on to promulgate His laws.[2] The living memory of His grace is considered the effectual grounds for obedience to His laws. Behind the prophetic threats and promises, the memory of this initiatory action of God looms, and the call to repentance stakes its hopes for realization upon the memory of that past event and the present action of divine sustenance, judgment, and redemption. In the New Testament the scene has changed with the coming of Jesus Christ, but the principle remains the same. Jesus' summary of the law and the prophets is not an isolated commandment.[3] The love of God and the neighbor presupposes the love of God, which on the one hand is universal, sending rain on the just and unjust, and which on the other hand is particular, in that He has continued faithful to His covenant people even when they have rebelled. Paul's letter to the Romans transfers the locus of God's prevenient action to

Christ when he writes, "God commandeth his own love toward us in that, while we were yet sinners, Christ died for us."[4] The First Epistle of John takes up the theme of grace and response: "We love, because he first loved us."[5] Thus in the very act of being confronted with God's establishment of man in a new relation, the whole horizon of man's ethical response is transformed. As all existence is a gift, as all moral commandments are at root signs of His care, and as men now see in and through Christ the fullness of God's love to them, so their response is made possible—a response not of grudging obedience to an external obligation laid down by a celestial tyrant but of a hearty, full-bodied, free streaming forth of life in gratitude, repentance, and faithful love to Him.[6] Indeed the motive power of a faith-ethic is, in essence, gratitude.

There is no longer a question of a rationalistic and legalistic deduction of ethical and religious regulations from an original principle, but the living outward from a new center of being. Nor is there a question of response being a kind of mechanical, calculated activity after an insight or revelation has been given. In one act, as it were, in the meeting with God through Christ, is both the activity of God apprehended and the transformation or conversion of the self effected. Faith gone to work in life is the direct and immediate result. So Luther could speak of faith as an energizing of the self to "good works" without thought to that dogged concentration upon the self and its virtues with which rationalistic ethics plagues humanity. Faith he described as "living, busy, active, mighty," ever productive of specific good works. By faith "a man is ready, and glad, without compulsion, to do good to everyone, to serve everyone, to suffer everything, in love and praise of God who has shown him his grace."[7] The "ought" is transformed or caught up into the "is" of grateful service and loving obedience. Obligation itself is no longer the distinctive and final category of morality. Love and gratitude, operating out of faith, have converted it.[8]

However, this understanding of the relation between divine action and faith does not eliminate the more prosaic elements of morality in daily life. The need for personal discipline is ever with us, though a life lived out of faith is one which is open to new needs and opportunities for growth in love.[9] The Christian life is not a static condition but a struggle and a process. Saints do not spring up overnight! The recalcitrant factors of mental sloth, ethical dullness, self-concern, and habitual practices continue to rear blockages to love's fulfillment. Nor does faith in some sudden, magical way provide us with information and solutions for dubious ethical situations. Bonhoeffer, in referring to the problem of "telling the truth," points up the imperative for the most careful examination of issues and circumstances in such cases. "Telling the truth," he comments, "is not solely a matter of moral character; it is also a matter of correct appreciation of real situations and of serious reflection upon them."[10] Faith and love know no moratorium on reason and experience. Hard grubbing for the facts and imaginative intelligence for drawing up hypotheses and conclusions cannot be by-passed in Christian morality. Consideration is a safeguard against spasmodic sentimentality or actions which do harm because they are not really directed to the good of the other person or situation.[11]

In the same way, where faith and love confront economic and political issues, which they must if they are not to wander off into vacuous and irrelevant preachments, there is the need for appraising these situations as realistically as possible and formulating appropriate plans for action. This constructive bridging of the gap between faith and the decisions which must be made in concrete situations J. H. Oldham and J. C. Bennett have called "middle axioms."[12] These "axioms" aim to incorporate the authentic note of response to God's demand and the empirical elements of the world's needs through which He meets us. In Bennett's words: "A 'middle axiom' is more concrete than a universal ethical principle and less specific than a program that includes legislation and political strategy."[13] As intermediary policies, "middle axioms" can never be identified with the divine will, nor can the action to which they lead be sanctified, as in legalism, by an extension of divine approval. Rather they are temporary, pragmatic structures molded to actual needs, not ideal possibilities, held under judgment of the love they never succeed in expressing completely but to which they point.[14] They are open to correction and extension not only in the light of fresh situations but in the light of new demands for righteousness which God lays upon men of sensitive insight. They make possible, and even necessary, corporate action with so-called secular moral forces, though in the two instances the motivations and standpoints of ultimate judgment may be quite different.

Repeatedly representative church groups and concerned individuals have worked out positions which may be called "middle axioms." These statements have seldom met with universal support and implementation within the Christian churches, yet they have often pointed to relevant, intermediate steps by which Christians and others may begin in a practical way to witness to the moral imperative of community. In the days when discussion was focused upon the establishment of the United Nations, the Commission on a Just and Durable Peace of the Federal Council of Churches set forth the following proposal: "The peace must provide the political framework for a continuing collaboration of the United Nations, and in due course, of neutral and enemy nations." As John Bennett has commented, this is not only a statement of a general principle about peace but a connection established with a definite, proposed organization and program. The proposal itself is not a program of action; it hovers between conviction and principle on the one hand and concrete recommendation on the other. In this sense it is a "middle axiom."

In discussing American foreign policy, Herman F. Reissig recently offered a "middle axiom" in this form: "Whatever the United States does or does not do about bomb testing, disarmament, negotiation of political disputes, our country has a clear obligation to strengthen its program of foreign economic aid and to help increase the flow of world trade." In the light of thorough and impartial studies by congressional and presidential committees which agreed on the value of foreign aid, Reissig feels justified in proposing the statement above. He obviously believes that his "axiom" joins Christian moral conviction and relevant good sense in terms of the potential contribution to world peace which such aid would offer. In a similar vein, Victor Obenhaus refers to the church's responsibility in race relations by tying the mandate of Christian brotherhood to the eradication of segregation, both within the churches and in American society. When Obenhaus deals with church-state problems, he again offers a "middle axiom" in this form: "Any religion or any interpretation of a single faith should thus be free to proclaim itself in the open market place of religious ideas."[15]

Efforts such as these, however, must be seen in the light of the total character of a faith ethic. If, as Buber has said, every ethos has its origin in a revelation, we must designate what this revelation means. Consistent with our statement of the form of the ethical question in the previous chapter, we hold that God both gives and asks something in our meeting with Him. Whatever it is He gives, He also asks of us. The demand cannot be dissociated from its rootage in the character of the ultimate. But both the gift and the demand must be appropriated by the person in faith. We have been found of that which is most worthy to claim our wholehearted allegiance, and we have been enabled to yield this devotion by the transformation of our existence in its depths. That which is given and appropriated has become the standard by which we estimate our success and failure as moral beings. In accepting our existence from the hands of God, we have also bound ourselves to the terms of our existence before Him. These terms, by our inward appropriation of them, are the claims which now we acquiesce in as normative for our existence. We admit their authority and legitimacy as the measure of our responsibility. We judge ourselves in the light of them. But since they come to us not merely as demands but filled with the content of God's action of love, we find in them substantial grounds for hope for redemption from our frailty and disobedience. What is revealed is not a principle or a truth abstractly considered but the beginning of a new life, "the new being," which is the earnest of what may yet be. At the same time the gift and the demand provide the basis of a unifying perspective upon the kaleidoscopic experiences of our existence. The shifting, disorderly, and seemingly random events of nature and human life are made intelligible by being brought into the scope of the revelation. We see ourselves and our world as one world under God's sovereignty, because we have already found a measure of unity in the revelatory experience itself. Thus faith provides the ground of intelligibility by offering to us an interpretative principle which emerges directly out of our existence as grounded in God.

What then shall we say of the content of this revelation? Without some identifiable content we have only stated above the form which revelation might take, if there were revelation! But as we have seen, revelation cannot be argued for any more than can faith. The proof, if such it could be called, lies in confession—confession not only in word but in transformed existence gone to work in the world. Yet a word must be found which does least injustice to the content of revelation, and which communicates least inadequately the profundity of the experience.

The word "love" first occurs as a suitable term. Probably no better word can be found to apply to the ultimate purpose and power of God. It stands for the highest manifestation of the divine will and the action of man which most fully expresses the human effort to effect reconciliation among persons. But love applies to that which is uniquely personal, whereas we seek a word which in its breadth of meaning can also do justice to the operation of God in the sub-personal spheres of nature and society. For this perhaps no term is more satisfactory than "community," if we conceive it broadly enough and show its implications clearly enough for the world of God's creation, for the entire world must in some way show forth the divine will.[16]

The word "community" has become a notoriously difficult one to define or explain in contemporary theological jargon. R. L. Calhoun, for example, describes it as a corporate group in which diversity, unity, freedom, and discipline are subtly related, all contributing to "the deep unity of life."[17] D. D. Williams regards community as "the order in which the members of a society are so related that the freedom, uniqueness, and power of each serves the freedom, uniqueness, and growth of all the other members."[18] Nels Ferré, expressing the divine ground of community explicitly, writes: "By community we mean a psychic social and spiritual reality rooted in God's activity in history. . . . Such community becomes more or less concrete in history."[19] Brunner confines the term to interpersonal relations because community for him involves free decision, peculiar only to man. Therefore, all that nature "knows as unity may be described as non-community."[20] Bultmann, while allowing that there is a kind of community "transmitted" by nature, puts his full weight also upon personal interrelatedness. He finds there are four forms which community assumes, the last of which genuinely fulfills his conception of the term: "the community transmitted by nature; the community which has developed in history; the community which has been founded by the intellectual world of art and science; the community founded by religion."[21] Each author in his own way supports Brunner's conclusion that "Man cannot be man 'by himself'; he can only be man in community. For love can only operate in community and only in this operation of love is man human."[22]

Suggestive as these and additional descriptions may be,[23] I shall begin at another point for the exposition of community. The central point is that of God's sovereign love, which binds together all beings into unity and mutual relatedness without diminution of their individual uniqueness and diversity. We begin by accepting not the nature of personality as determinative for community but the unity which God gives in the creation of this world as one world, and the pressure to unity which is exhibited in its relevant forms at every level of His world. Faith sees "community" as one way of expressing the fact that, wherever and whenever God acts, the ultimate aim is His glorification, carried out by both giving and pressing for the maximum interrelation among all beings while safeguarding the diversity of each. Thus, first of all, community is not simply a human possibility devised for personal self-fulfillment alone. It is His act by which particular beings may exist at all—that is, by the integrity of their being—and by which they may be meaningfully related to each other in the integrity of their being. Being is dependent on structural unity; to be is to participate in community. While on the one hand we say with Bultmann that faith "brings to light the hidden community of all men," by virtue of which they exist as persons, we must equally insist with Brunner that "All that actually exists, in spite of the gulf which lies between 'this' and 'that,' is connected existence."[24] Thus we cast the net of community over a wider range of existence than that comprehended in personal community, though without, we hope, doing injustice to the latter. If divine sovereignty be taken with seriousness, nothing less than the whole range of God's world can be accepted as exhibiting His will to community, and nothing less can be the limit of man's peculiar opportunity and obligation for community. If all creation speaks to faith of this undergirding community, at the same time it lays claim upon our concern, appreciation, and responsibility to it. If God by His creation and sustenance loves the world, must one not also love and cherish that which is His?[25]

In its most general form, the term "community" designates the reality which faith holds to be the will of God. Community signifies His way of creating, sustaining, judging, and redeeming His creation. Behind all the terms which express the variety and differences within being, such as "here" and "there," "this" and "that," "separation," "uniqueness," "identity," and even "guilt" and "sin" on the personal level, there lies the comprehensive unity by virtue of which we are enabled to speak intelligibly of these distinctions. Behind every attempt at communication, from the most meager mutual influences of matter to the sophisticated discourse of persons, this presupposition of relationality holds. To take up the theme of Colossians, all things hold together in Him, and without Him there would be only chaos, if that! Community is the way of existence, no matter how often broken or infringed upon. Although it comes to most precious and richest fulfillment in personal relations, faith will not accept the notion that God casts outside His care and sustenance any segment of His creation, even nature. From our limited human standpoint, we may not be able to see in any clear fashion what forms of community God wills in and among the parts of nature, but neither can we deny to nature its part in His creation, nor our intimate relation to it. Human community cannot be used as the prototype of all community. Each level of existence must have its own characteristic expression, though these are observed from the standpoint of persons.

The life of Christian faith, in the light of the more inclusive meaning of community, is one lived in awareness of the total context in which human life emerges and develops. Whether or not we choose to call our relation to nature and God morality is a relatively unimportant matter. What is essential is the appreciation and responsibility the Christian feels and undertakes as created being in the framework of God's sovereign will to community. Thus we have set before us the question of what community means specifically in respect to a life lived in the presence of nature, society, and the personal encounters to which the term "love" properly belongs. Let us attempt to trace out some of the implications which community has in these three settings.

Many contemporary theologians have emphasized the fact that man becomes fully personal only in relation to other persons. Personality presupposes distinctively human society. Sometimes, however, it has escaped our notice that man becomes man also by virtue of his participation in nature. This participation in nature is a strange kind of experience for man, because he is both within nature yet set apart from it. One of the most basic distinctions we make as we mature as persons is that between personal selves and the world of animals, plants, rivers, and mountains. If we treat the realm of nature as though it were but an extension of human consciousness, we run off into childish animism and superstition. But if we treat it as something completely alien to ourselves, we fall into the opposite danger of attempting to live on what is sometimes called "the spiritual plane," denying our rootage in the physical at times, even to the point of savage asceticism. Yet we are bound to nature, and nature does not let us go. Nor do we ever truly conquer it. We work through nature, even when we try to control or dominate it.

We are born of copulation. We are sustained by the orderly behavior of stones, molecules, and cells in the aggregate. Indeed, we would not exist in any recognizable sense except for the structural processes of nature. Yet we are distinct from nature as selves who can turn upon nature to ponder its ways, who can reflect upon ourselves and can make use of its energies. Human culture derives from the recognition and practical implementation of this dual relation of participation in and transcendence to nature.[26]

This dual relation of man with nature makes possible a unique type of communion with nature which is nowhere else found in the total range of the meaning of community. We can rise to heights of empathetic relation with nature which are unparalleled in any known form of personal community, yet we can never be submerged in the flow of its elemental powers, since we are persons, not merely animated segments of nature.

Faith accepts and rejoices in the communion with nature which God makes possible by giving nature and man a common meeting ground and in so doing addressing us in a powerful new way. We are deeply and mysteriously moved by wheeling stars, yawning interstellar spaces, a storm at sea, the grace of golden aspens against a clean blue sky, the majesty of a mountain, or the flight of wild geese across a November sky. We are caught up in wonder and awe by the intricate subtleties revealed by the electronic microscope, the teeming life of a square foot of garden space, the birth of a child, or even the operation of our mental faculties.

As Leslie Hunter puts it, "Much of the little in me which seems to have the quality of eternity and which seems least in need of purification and reform, is the power to be in harmony with and to enjoy earth and water, wood and rock—the stuff of this earth which we apprehend through our senses. These and I are of the same stuff. In the infinite variety of shape, colour, and fragrance which there is upon this globe, and which far exceeds in wonder and beauty all the works of man, both pious and secular—in these shapes, colours, and fragrances of the natural world, my whole being rejoices."[27] Such is the living mystery for which no product of human hands or human companionship is a substitute—where God speaks directly through His creation, untouched and untamed by man's wit or sin.

If we are to believe some modern philosophers, even nature itself does not hold completely aloof from some response to human action. The animal world is made up not of automatons but of incipiently self-conscious creatures which respond to gestures, commands, and perhaps even moods. And deeper in nature, it has been suggested, there is a realm where relations and events occur in curious sensitivity to each other—more on the analogy of an organism than on that of a smoothly operating machine.[28]

Yet even if these speculations prove futile, nature remains in the authenticity of its own being a creature of God. Here in nature faith recognizes not an order simply to be subdued to our use or exploitation but a reality of its own with a claim upon God's concern no less important than our own. By its mysterious presence it reminds us that God has purposes beyond or different from those of human salvation, that He has willed us to live out of and with nature as the ground of our physical and aesthetic existence. To live with this world as God's world is then to be opened to horizons of thought and imagination which stretch the coiled interests of the self or of humanity. One who has felt the pulsating power of this encounter with nature can never settle quietly within the circumference of his own problems and comforts.[29]

The world of nature also has its way of mutely laying responsibilities upon us, not in its own right, but by virtue of its place in the world which God loves. In the forest fire carelessly started, the thoughtless exhaustion of precious topsoil, or the pollution of streams and lakes, man breaks roughly into the economy of nature, destroying its balance. Our cruelty to animals and the wanton destruction of natural beauties are condemnable, not simply in the light of man's enlightened self-interest, but on the deeper basis of faith's conviction that "the earth is the Lord's, and the fullness thereof." "Sparrows and sheep and lilies belong within the network of moral relations where God reveals himself," as H. R. Niebuhr says. "Now every killing is a sacrifice; the culture of the earth as a garden of the Lord and reverence for the stars as creatures of his intelligence belong to the demands of the universal will."[30]

Nature in yet another aspect assumes the character of the sacramental, the vehicle of God's meeting with man in peace or judgment.[31] Amos cries out that the Lord roars from Zion—and nature shrivels and withers before His mighty blast. Second Isaiah intones the mercy of God seen in the making of the hills low, the valleys listen, and the way made straight and plain for the returning exile. In the cloud by day and the pillar of fire by night He leads His people out of bondage toward the Promised Land. The material elements of the Lord's Supper may both reveal and conceal the God of Jesus Christ, though never in such a way as to replace His revelation through Jesus Christ.[32] Yet when God speaks to us through nature, He does so in such a way as to convince us that He is Lord of this realm, not we; that it lives and pulsates by the breath of life which He alone has breathed into it. Thus His revelation through nature is itself an indispensable sign of His sovereignty. It may be a rebuke to our anxious, self-centered concern about our own salvation. It may bring a fresh awareness of our need of salvation from that divorcement between body and spirit which is the sign of our refusal to accept nature into our own existence.

To some the intelligible structure of our universe may bespeak the creative ordering and sustaining work of God. For others the hurricane, flood, fallen sparrow, and the grass of the field tell of His awesome power, the hiddenness of His purposes, and His objectivity as He stands over against us. At times, for some, nature quiets and soothes in its apparent serenity and placidity. Or again it lures us to a disquietude by calling up unspeakable yearnings, as it lengthens to unimaginable limits the horizons of our finite time. The boisterous action of elemental forces may shake us in fear, yet strangely elevate us—as they did Edwards while he watched and listened to the thunderstorms roll about the hills of the Connecticut valley. At such moments the sense of the majesty of God breaks through, subduing us in awe, but lifting us to praise and worship of the Lord of Lords. Not even our scientific knowledge replaces this profound awareness of God's glory in nature, set against our comparative insignificance. By the unleashing of these natural powers may come "the fear of the Lord" which is the beginning of all wisdom. As one modern author suggests, "the fear of nature is not based upon one's ignorance of nature, but upon one's knowledge of himself in the face of nature."[33] So in nature we may be called down from the high place of self-esteem as well as lifted up from the shrill naggings, folly, and cruelty of our competitive existence with our fellow men. God both bids us approach Him, yet holds us at arm's length. In massive power and majesty He stands over against us as both the lure to our fulfillment and the untamed reality in whose presence we must constantly live. He calls us to communion with Himself through nature, but never to personal intimacy or absorption in the fullness of His being.

Faith recognizes no form of pantheism as a suitable expression for its encounter with God through nature. Indeed, God is near to us in nature, but He is not identified with it. Nature is itself but created, finite being, offering therefore no ultimate resting place for our faith. It has its own unique existence under God, its own way to go. It can neither be collapsed into the universal mind and being of God, nor can it encompass in turn the totality of the divine existence. In a like manner it cannot be folded into our human consciousness nor engulf it into itself. God apparently wills its existence as it is, finite, with its own obdurate forms of being. And this is why we may take exception to the suggestion of Buber that human meetings with natural objects may be construed in the personal relation of the "I-Thou" idiom. Trees, stars, clouds, worms, birds, and all the rest have their own authenticity of being, which human categories must accept, not transform. Impersonal objects are not persons, nor vice versa, and we but confound ourselves and human knowledge when we attempt to understand either in terms of the other. It may be speculated, without impiety we hope, that if God had wanted trees, storms, clouds, etc., treated as "thous" He would have made them such. And it is, furthermore, always dangerous to treat the knowledge relation as a causal one in which the knower so radically transforms the character of the object known as to change its metaphysical status. The tendency of the "I-Thou" type of thinking, when applied to nature, lies precisely in this direction. An aesthetic or personalistic monism reduces the realm of nature to an extension of personalistic relations, thereby erasing the substantial uniqueness of nature's forms and confusing the categories of the personal and impersonal. But such seems to be the outcome of Buber's far-flung usage of the "I-Thou" relation.[34] Communion with God through nature honors the reality of the vehicle without identifying it with either the personal or the divine. Without its impersonal form, it could not serve as the particular type of vehicle and evidence of God's integrative activity which it is for faith.

This strange world of nature, to which we stand in paradoxical community, rears up in the independent authenticity of its own character to speak for itself. It is as though it refuses to be considered merely as a link between God and man, or an object of aesthetic contemplation or exploitation by man. Indeed, if it is to speak as a revelation of God, it must speak to us of itself, for is it

not also within the orbit of divine sustenance, judgment, and reconciling concern in its own right?

In our deepest communion with nature, we catch an intimation,
though nothing more, of its pathos and hope—if we may use the
words. Nature bears a secret of its own which we can only acknowl-
edge, but never fully understand. It is a realm darkened by the
mute impress of an unfulfilled good. It is riddled with fear, sordid
waste, and rot, cruelty and competitive bloody struggle. Over it
hangs a "tragic flaw" of some kind, a melancholy, unexpressed
frustration which is woven into its impassive orderliness. The fallen
sparrow, trampled flower, wounded and dying animal, seared leaf of
autumn, the stunted tree, the passing star—all bespeak the power
of a ruinous severity which flails about, regardless of beauty or
possible fulfillment. Something has gone awry in nature itself; it
bears a wound, that of unrealized community within itself.[35]

Marcel's comment upon nature is no mawkish or sentimental
one. "It seems to me," he writes, "that any study of the notion of
created Nature, which is fundamental for the Christian, leads to
the conclusion that there is in the depth of Nature, as of reason
which is governed by it, a fundamental principle of inadequacy
to itself which is, as it were, a restless anticipation of a different
order."[36] And this is a conviction which has long played a part
in Hebraic and Christian thought, though often suppressed in
favor of our sole interest in human salvation.

The overtones of this drama of nature are heard in the Genesis
myths of creation and fall. An idyllic harmony founded in creation
is lost in the divine judgment to the detriment of not only man but
earth and animal world as well. The conflict between man and soil,
man and the beasts, takes its toll from nature no less than from
man. A curse lowers over all.

But this scene of man and nature ruptured from their common
relation is not the last word. From afar off the prophet Isaiah sees
the era of reconciliation coming—an age of bucolic peace with the
old bloody antagonisms gone, not only between man and nature,
but within nature itself. "Then the wolf will lodge with the lamb,
and the leopard will lie down with the kid; the calf and the young
lion will graze together, and a little child will lead them."[37] The
new age which the Jewish apocalyptists saw ahead was one in
which earth had resumed its spontaneous fruitfulness, with grapes
of such magnificent proportions that only a few of them would be

needed to make enormous quantities of wine! But the time was not yet fulfilled for such extravagant hopes to come true. We find Paul, therefore, sounding the theme of a whole creation, groaning and laboring painfully for redemption, a deliverance from the bondage of corruption which would soon appear.[38] Christian apocalyptic hopes meet the problem of nature's affliction with the vision of an old heaven and earth passed away and a new heaven and earth come.[39] Colossians sees in Christ the one who will reconcile all things "whether on earth or in heaven" unto himself and God.[40] And who can forget the gentle Francis of Assisi who caught up into his "Canticle to the Sun" the movement of all creation into a redemptive unity of love?

So in their respective ways these pronouncements of faith note the agony and frustration of nature, yet look beyond it to that community in which nature and man will be reconciled in such a way that each is the recipient of divine grace and promise, without detraction from the other. We know not the cause or the depth of nature's hurt, though often enough we experience its consequences in our own bodies. By faith alone can we trust and hope that He who has created nature, and ourselves with it in most profound attachment, purposes as redeemer some better thing than that wherewith both are now afflicted.

Whatever degree of community man finds and achieves with nature remains problematical. The superb aloofness by which man is lifted and enthralled proves also to be the quality by which he is kept outside the circle of nature's deepest secrets. The low degree of responsiveness with which nature greets man—to some entirely imperceptible—rebuffs him and sends him back to his own kind. Nature has a way of her own to travel, and it coincides only in part with our own. God's call to communion with nature, and to communion with Himself through nature, faith finds irreplaceable. But it is not the fullness of community which God continues to give and command in human relations. As He is Lord of nature and meets us there, drawing us to Himself yet humbling us in His confrontation, so also as Lord of history He gives human community as the foundation of personal existence, presses for its realization among men, and judges us in our failure to respond fully to its possibilities. So all human community remains the gift and the task given to men by Him who wills to bring us to Himself in a richness of community of which our own is but a pale facsimile.

Faith discerns in the most commonplace forms of man's social existence the evidence of the divine will to community. By institutions, traditions, customs, laws, speech, and the cultural products of the human spirit and hands, men reach out for each other, thereby publicly announcing each his lack of self-sufficiency, his need for others. He lives in an intricate network of relations with his contemporaries; he is immersed in the unceasing stream of social influences from the past; his life flows forward into the lives of the unborn. He can never know personally the many individuals who constitute his past, present, or future. Yet the decisions and acts of those past and present form the tough structure within which his life is lived, as his choices and acts in turn affect the fabric of society for his contemporaries and posterity. He assumes the burden of past evils and errors; he enjoys the benefits of the past as well. He pours his own mistakes, pains, and blessings into the common hoard, even as he lives out of it.[41] He finds himself thrown into accidental connections with persons with whom apparently he has little in common, save for loyalty to this or that transient cause. But from these tangential connections may grow profound personal involvements, responsibilities, and appreciations. Whether these allegiances and duties prove to be superficial or deeply moving, society through them gets its work done, and in the process persons develop. States are governed; armies move and fight; scientific research is carried out; goods are produced, sold, and bought; education proceeds; lodges, unions, and churches are formed; drama, art, and music come to expression.

Man's need for man, however, is by no means a sufficient guarantee of social harmony or of his just treatment of his fellows. Society hangs together not simply because we are fulfilled in and through others. Its measure of unity is compounded of our need for self-confirmation, fear, and the presence of law behind which stand both majesty and coercion. The struggle for advantage over others, the yearning for power concentrated in organizations which in turn determine policy affecting the lives of millions, is an ever present factor in society. The fundamental thrust to community is repeatedly shunted aside and distorted by those egoisms which recognize and bow only to the counterpressures of law, organized public opinion, and, in the last resort, force itself. Community is therefore always in a precarious state. It must be earned and fought for in the thick of society's tensions and crosscurrents. Faith sees the imperative of community laying an obligation upon Christians to use power responsibly and to hold under the judgment of community all uses of power, including that which the Christian himself may wield.

We live between the all-pervasive will to community, without which society is an impossibility, and the threat of coercion, without which society would be defenseless against brutality and chaos. The meeting point of these two elements, seldom exactly found and always precariously maintained, is justice embodied in law. Without an abiding and almost unconscious sense of participation of each in the other, law easily becomes imposed tyranny. Without the approximate justice of law and the coercion it implies, community is itself endangered. The power-seekers in the form of pressure groups, or individuals, find community too fragile a reality to check their depredations, when it is not balanced and preserved by law. And even "decent" people jeopardize community when in their limited social imaginations they identify the virtues of these smaller, less inclusive groups with the ultimate demand of full human community. Certainly man cannot and does not live on a straight diet of enacted laws, but neither can his complex common life be entrusted to the spontaneous desire for harmonious self-fulfillment, or to a dull, unthinking obedience to custom and tradition.

Human society is a form of community which in turn can provide a basis for the development of the more intimate forms of personal community. Society affords the field in which this personal community can flourish and can protect whatever measure of mutual participation may be achieved. In itself society is a realization of community but its nature can never be accepted by Christian faith as a final criterion of community. It is too ambiguous a mixture of coercion, self-interest, as well as mutuality, to serve as the universal standard of the divine will.

Having admitted this much, however, there is much more to be said for society as a form of and demand for community. Not every form of community must be of the personal type, and it is society which teaches us that the relatively impersonal structures in which human life is lived can be vehicles for the service of community. There are such things as monarchies, democracies, oligarchies, slavery, unionism, systems of law, business organizations which have their distinctive patterns of operation. These are part and parcel of what we mean by social structures which govern and influence human life, although they function with a minimum of face-to-face personal relations.[42] In our complex, technological culture, not a little of the service we perform for each other must of necessity pass through channels from which the personal factor has been almost excluded. Often the crucial beneficial act is carried out in those moments when the opportunity for personal confrontation is at a minimum, or in fact ought to be so. At certain times the "I-Thou" relation must be subordinated to the "I-It" relation if the relevant acts in the service of community in the deeper sense are to be performed.

On the operating table, I want the surgeon to be as "impersonal" as possible, as detached from personal involvement with me as possible, so he can the better carry out his responsibility of saving my life. In a time of danger, when order is the only hope of escape from fire or drowning, I see the need of being treated as anonymously as possible, as the sixth or tenth one to go out by a certain exit or enter the lifeboat. I want the professor to teach me anatomy, history, physics, etc., in the classroom, rather than to engage in probing my psyche. While playing a Beethoven quartet, I must subordinate my personal identity in the corporate unity of the group, in devotion to the music if the quartet is to be well played. I do not think the purpose of a symphonic concert well served if my attention is repeatedly drawn to the eccentricities of the conductor or the rosy hues of the face of the trombone player, or if my mind is filled with the thought "What a great composer or orchestra I am hearing." The personal factor, strictly speaking, ought to retire, that the music itself may stand forth in its own right. If I am ever going to get beyond the superficial level of listening to particular instrumentalists, conductors, or composers and analyzing structures, cadences and shadings, I must be brought at last, by human means to be sure, into the presence of the music itself. In the case of government, my initial and in some ways my most basic safeguard against arbitrariness and injustice is not the personality of any one legislator, judge, or executive but the law itself. I look to a government by law, not by persons, as the guardian of my rights and for the foundation of certain of my political and social duties. So when the Scottish theologian Buchanan argued for a government of law to curtail the royal prerogatives, he did so on the principle that the impersonality of law would make the king immune to the temptation of whimsical and capricious exercise of authority.[43] (Let me hastily add that no law makes anyone "immune" to injustice, nor does law prove a final safeguard against injustice!) Then there are those daily business "contacts"—and that is what they are, mere "contacts," "touchings" of one by another. In a trivial way, we may suggest that some of these contacts should be kept at the impersonal level. When I wish to purchase some intimate articles in a drugstore, I do not wish a highly personal conversation with the clerk on their prospective uses. I prefer him to serve me as a clerk, not as a medical adviser or a father confessor.

Hope Nicholson, in a remarkable article written after her recovery from mental illness, makes an unforgettable observation on the relation between the doctors and her condition.

> I think it must be a bit like a period in a political prison. If you knew at the time that you would be released in two years, that the world still wagged outside, and normal life would return, it would have been more bearable; but isolated and despairing, you did not know.

> Here, I suppose, comes in the virtue of hope, or faith. I went for six months' voluntary treatment to a mental hospital . . . and I think one valuable result of it was that it gave me just this faith. To the doctors there my private hell was just part of the daily round. They charted it with ease, I recovered, and I hope it will never present quite the same menace again.[44]

For one person, at least, the very air of confidence and impersonality with which her deeply private and agonizing experience was treated served as a primary agent of recovery.

We are driven to recognize that community as society is characterized by the double realities of the "institution" and the "role." These two appear to be, within limits, the expression of the deep thrust to community of which faith makes us aware, but they do not bear the full weight of the term "community" as employed in a Christian context. The impersonal aspect of the institution can be observed by the way persons are treated within it. They are replaceable; their roles often are not. Thus in the American form of government a president is necessary, but not a particular person as president. In law, a judge and a lawyer are necessary—but not these particular men. In case of fire, we call for firemen, not particular firemen. The structure goes on, but persons come and go. They are replaceable. We obviously cannot derive from such an arrangement of society the notion of "the infinite value of human personality." If we look about us at our institutional life, we soon see how futile it is to argue anything from it regarding personal value. Certain institutional forms give play for personality, but they do not establish the priority or the value of persons as such. At best they can only presuppose it. Yet even in this case persons are "used," are "substituted" for each other, or "supplant" each other, as the circumstances dictate. The ground of the value of persons must lie not in a state, an economic order, a family, even, but only in the recognition, which passes beyond the empirical, that God creates, sustains, judges, and redeems men, that is, He values them. Their value is not derivative from society in any forms which it assumes; it lies with God Himself.

Perhaps it is because men are replaceable in institutions that they often either attach themselves to institutions with a fierce desperation or abandon responsibility for or to them. On the one hand, the institution—if it be sweeping enough in its claims, and powerful enough to make them good—stands for much that individual men covet for themselves. It stands for stability and safety amid change; purpose in the midst of the random and chaotic; and association, if not community, with others in the emptiness of atomistic individualism. The larger impersonal structures such as the state, the business corporation, and even the church, gather to themselves the aura of divine mystery and sanction before which men bend. They appear like eternity in the midst of time, and there are those among us who surrender gladly to their claims. The impressive drama, pomp and ceremony, the "credenda" and "miranda" of their power, swell the human heart in exultation at the prospect of identification with them. On their altars private ambitions are immolated for the sake of the "cause." In their names the noblest deeds are avowed, the most execrable atrocities are forgiven. We lose ourselves for "them" and "their" wills, and count it no loss, if we but be swept up into the glory of their fathomless purposes.

On the other hand, when men realize that they are replaceable and expendable in institutions, they may revolt to the opposite course. The massive structure of a state, a business corporation, or a "universal" church is too remote and unfeeling to capture their imaginations. They are repelled by the remoteness, the "facelessness," and the outward symbols of authority. The impersonality of the institution does not evoke devotion; it only loosens and makes indefinite one's moral responsibility. It is a world which belongs to no one in particular, where there is no moral blame or responsibility. The state acts, not I. I am not the state. The state is "it" or "they"—

which we never see. "It" or "they" own property, issue orders, pass and execute laws, but they never come close to us. They are abstractions, or lumpish, unmanageable things that somehow loom up about us but never take on concrete recognizable form. They are impalpable, but there in fact. We have no personal responsibility for them or to them. Their property is not ours; we may treat it as vandals. Their claims issue from no one in particular, so we attempt to evade them. The anonymous can claim no moral response from us. We go our own way—if we can!

Thus the impersonal in human society may be overvalued and absolutized to the point of idolatry or demonolatry, crushing out the imagination and freedom of persons. Mere collectivity, the distortion of community, takes over, and in Brunner's colorful phrase, the individual "is regarded merely as so much compost to enrich the cultural dung-heap."[45] In the other direction, personhood is dissipated by surrender to chaotic, irresponsible impulse. The denial of the value of the impersonal structures leads, no less than does fanatical subservience to them, to the annihilation of man as man, that is, man in community with other men and God. Yet by the impersonal may community be served within the framework of organized society.

Men are not only drawn together in institutions; they are given their tasks to perform in institutions by the roles they assume. The role is not simply the vocation we take up; it is the characteristic way in which society determines and channels our vocations. The role is both an expression of the person in his social relations and a concealment and perhaps even a distortion of the person. It is a mode of acting which the individual seldom invents but which tradition, custom, and the total structure of a society demand. So we meet each other less as authentic persons in our own right than as husbands, wives, tradesmen, businessmen, lawyers, judges, engineers, artists, soldiers, authors, class or race members, and the like. We may assume any one or a combination of these roles, sometimes freely, sometimes by training and indoctrination. And we identify ourselves with these roles in varying degrees of intensity.

Our roles are the masks we wear, but they are peculiar masks, for they both hide us from others and express us to others. We may chafe under the mask, but we also recognize it as a means of self-expression, as a way of achieving security in a securely approved status, and as a method of serving basic human needs. We are embarrassed by those who would strip us of our roles and expose us "as we really are," yet we are glad not to be identified with any one role too closely. The role is in some sense what we "really" are, but it is never the whole story of what we are. The comparatively impersonal status of a role protects and expresses the growing self, but it changes and controls its growth. It enables us to enmesh ourselves into the world's work, and thereby respond to the concrete demand of God, but it lays its own ethos upon us, demanding services and acts which by no means make manifest our allegiance to the divine will. It opens us toward others, giving opportunities for relations with them we would never otherwise have; it closes us off from others, giving us a secret place to hide from the eyes of others.

As in the case of the institution, faith sees the role as the necessary but not final means of expression of community. It may protect our self-interest, our scramble for prestige and power; it may cloak our cruelty and impassiveness toward other persons.[46] It offers limitless possibilities for practicing that inward duplicity in which to some degree we all exist, the divorcement between the self and its acts, while all the time, to the eye of the observer, we may perform with poise the amenities of civilized courtesy. Such is the troubling thought which Walt Whitman expressed in his *Leaves of Grass*:

> Behold a secret silent loathing and despair.
> No husband, no wife, no friend, trusted to hear this confession,
> Another self, a duplicate of every one, skulking and hiding it goes,
> Formless and wordless through the streets of the cities, polite and
>   bland in the parlours,
>
> . . . .
>
> Smartly attired, countenance sunburn'd, form upright, death under
>   the breast-bones, hell under the skull bones . . .
> Keeping fair with the customs, speaking not a syllable of itself,
> Speaking of anything else but never of itself.[47]

Yet for faith, the carrying out of the roles which our institutional life makes necessary need be no hypocritical farce. It may be the opportunity we have for promoting community within the limits of our abilities and the scope of the institutional role. It ties us down to the here and now, calling upon us for definite contributions of service to humanity's need. It provides the materials with which ethical insight and spiritual stamina grapple. It is the means by which we stand in interdependence with one another; it is itself the response to the undergirding interdependence in which God has created us. It shields and directs the growing self, giving it form and structure. Therefore, the deeper claim of community does not call for a kind of spiritual nudity, a reckless casting off of one's roles in the name of emancipation. Rather we are called upon to live with fidelity in our various roles, if they be of social benefit. This is a fidelity which finds its justification, not in the demands of the roles themselves, but in the supreme allegiance one holds to the divine by faith. Fidelity is defined not in terms of faithful obedience to the role itself but in respect to the ultimate ground of faith, which calls us to faithful service in and through the role. We are called to live with a sensitive imagination to the creative possibilities which come with our roles, so they shall become tools, not masters, of community. The self with its roles must be open continuously to the influence of God's transformative love.

So when we look back upon the part which these impersonal elements play in relation to community, we see them not as unworthy evidence of God's will to community. Our institutions, roles, causes, associations, lodges, clubs, traditions, etc., are not inherently depersonalizing. They evidence instead the way we are created for each. They point toward community in its fullest sense of personal relation; they support personal community, giving it opportunity to flourish. But when the impersonal falls under the domain of sin, as it does repeatedly, it shocks us with its heinous consequences. Then the personal authenticity is ruthlessly stamped out; freedom is lost; imagination is stereotyped; brutality is justified; and man in his deepest being as a child of God is voided of all significance. And this is why the man of faith is called to the tension of living in and with the impersonal, yet never succumbing to its insidious possibilities for negating the Lordship of God and the value of the personal. He lives with the insistent claim of a God who is Lord over the relatively unchanging structures of society but who nevertheless changes and judges them, showing up their finitude and impermanence. He lives with a God who wills, by His free gift of love to man, that man meet Him in freedom. And what stands in the way of that free communion stands also condemned by the highest tribunal.

Even put in the most sympathetic light, the life of society, life as a member of a group, institution, collectivity, or in a role, leaves us with the sober fact of the replaceability of individual persons. Men are expended and used; they are not treasured for what they are in their own uniqueness. Moreover, they come together in such a haphazard, accidental way that their relations are bound to be superficial.[48] Yet we cannot live satisfactorily out of these surface connections; we cannot force ourselves without remainder into our diverse roles. We cry out for a fullness of commitment to other persons, and they for us, for which the impersonal does not allow. Without personal meeting, without personal love, it is not too dramatic to say we die. We must love and be loved; we cannot go on being "replaceable" units. Without love we die, first on the fringes of the spirit's sensitivity, but finally deep in the heart of our being, when we know we are unwanted and valueless except for the moment. In faith, we say, God wills us to be for each other in love, the level of personal community.

"God has created man to be a self, an individual, but He did not create him to be alone, to live for and by himself."[49] This is the double truth out of which personal or existential community grows. On the one hand stands the indissoluble uniqueness of the individual self with its intelligence, freedom, responsibility, and its own personal history; on the other hand, the need for fulfillment through other unique selves, yet never in such a way as to make other selves mere agencies of one's own fulfillment. In the delicate balance between these two foci, personal community or the "I-Thou" relation is established. As Schleiermacher put it: "Enter into community in such a way as to keep your individuality intact; cultivate individuality in such a way that in so doing you also enter into community."[50]

Community of this type is not lightly or speedily entered. The self must first understand itself before God as an isolated self, a self which bears the scars of disunity from God and man but which knows itself fatefully bound to God in a way in which it is neither bound to itself nor to any human being. The encounter of faith "first of all tears man out of every human community and places him in radical loneliness before God."[51]

In this situation of loneliness before God is grounded the irreplaceable uniqueness of each of us. Here we realize, sometimes with terror, that we are not mere samples of the human species or products of social conditioning. We are called to this particular selfhood which is ours—and it would in some instances be unbearable were it not that we are met in faith by the God of mercy who accepts us as we are.[52] Uniqueness and personal authenticity stem from this depth relation, but not independence. In place of independence is born freedom—freedom to be ourselves without let or hindrance from any person or association of men; freedom to enter into attachments and community with others. And, as bound to God in freedom, we are claimed for responsibility for ourselves and others. The authentic, free, and responsible self is then one of the absolutely essential bases faith finds for the higher levels of community. Of this personal authenticity, the "mass" or "crowd" knows nothing, for it cherishes only the "replaceable," the "malleable," and the "anonymous."

Isolation or loneliness does not signify a turning to individualism. The individual is established as an individual in isolation before God, but isolation always refers by implication to that from which one is separated. To be isolated is to be set over against something or someone to which we belong. It is the privation of a connection whose memory lingers on in loneliness, coloring it with poignancy and yearning; not only a memory, but a hope that the last good may be restored—the communion with God and one's fellow men. If the "I" is established by God in loneliness, no less is the "We" and the "Thou" set before us as that from which we have been separated and estranged, and to which we long to return.

"Shame," Bonheffer describes in a striking passage, is "man's ineffaceable recollection of his estrangement from the origin; it is grief for this estrangement, and the powerless longing to return to unity with the origin." When we lower our eyes in meeting a stranger and do not sustain his gaze with our own, is this "a sign of that shame, which, when it knows it is seen, is reminded of something that it lacks, namely, the lost wholeness of life, its own nakedness"? Is this the reason we enter with ambivalence into personal relations? Aware of the prodigious abyss which separates us from every other person, yet stirred by a memory or a hope of reconciliation, we live "between covering and discovering, between self-concealment and self-revelation, between solitude and fellowship."[53]

Yet personal community flourishes between the human "I" and "Thou" because of both the separation and the common memory and hope. Travelers from a common land, they recognize each other in a foreign country. As those are drawn to each other who have passed through a similar danger or happiness, so are those who meet fully in community. They bear the scars of being called to free and responsible selfhood; they know the healing in which personal estrangement is transcended. Each has dignity, not as the accidental fortunes of class, race, individual success, or endowment dictate, but as the free gift of God calls to them to be His and each other's. The human "I" and "Thou" weave between them the subtle, precious tapestry of mutual understanding and gracious affection as the response to His patient understanding and love. Entering into each other's lives intimately, they create a new life which, while it enriches the life of each in its own right, transcends the lives of both as an object of loyalty and a criterion of judgment.

General definitions and descriptions of this personal community prove weak and pallid when compared to the vibrant power of the relation itself.[54] It is a fellowship of free selves where the selves are bound together by common concerns and purposes, so that there is a maximum of joyful mutual acceptance and a maximum of serious judgment. Without the full acceptance of the other, we would have only carping criticism; without judgment and discrimination in respect to the other, we would have only sentimental alliance. The "two" must hold together, accepting and loving in such a way that each knows he is valued for himself, with all his faults and follies, yet judged in such a manner that he understands he is not loved either *for* his faults or *in spite of* them, but *in* the faults which at any given moment are part of him. Mutual affection holds the two selves together; it treasures the possibilities of the other and imaginatively seeks new forms of expression for them. Judgment seizes upon those factors which prevent and distort the fuller meeting of the "I" and "Thou"; it criticizes and corrects them in the light of the higher possibility of community, and in so doing cleanses the relation of the superficial and egocentric. Only in love are we free to judge each other and to accept the judgment of another without rankling memory; thus love becomes responsible. We are free to forgive and be forgiven; thus responsibility is tempered with mercy and tenderness.

To live in such a relation calls for openness of the self to another. It brings enlargement and expansion of conscience. But this is an openness practiced within security. We are free to be open with each other because we fully accept and judge each other with no thought of taking advantage of the deep mutual knowledge we gain. We can reveal, not conceal, we can expose, not hide from each other because we trust each other. We can know relief from holding in our darkest secret and most extravagant hopes. By the same token of openness in trustfulness, we invite the confidence and self-revelation of the other. So we are genuinely available to each other without that nagging duplicity of mind and heart which mars so much human intercourse. We are not looking past the other, hoping to catch the eye of some more "interesting" or "important" person who can help us scramble up the ladder of success. We are mindful of this person before us; we desire to meet him fully, and to do that we must be there before him fully. "More powerful and more holy than all writing is the presence of a man who is simply and directly there," as Buber says.[55]

In these moments of openness and availability we not only listen to the spoken word. We read the facial expression, catch the fleeting inflection of the voice, and interpret the furtive gesture. A background of hidden understandings and meanings is being woven between us, one which enables us to enter with ever increasing sensitivity and insight into each other's lives. So gradually, often painfully, we come together in fidelity, participating in the memory of shared events of the past, contributing to a growing history of mutual regard which withstands the strain of self-interest. In a measure, this is redemption, for in our larger common history we are saved from the meagerness of our own past experiences and from the pitiable narrowness with which self-concern persistently threatens human existence.

Community, however, is redemptive in another sense. It is the locus of truth, the place where each can be for the other without dissimulation. It offers the opportunity for living out the integrity, the purpose of one's being, because we are met by the other who is daring to do the same. In the atmosphere of mutual availability and fidelity we not only can speak the truth of ourselves, so far as human words can encompass it; we can enact and live out truth by being faithful to the needs of the other. Personal truth can emerge only in such a setting of openness and fidelity, for the truth is the relation itself, not the statement of either one or the other. We are "true" to each other and to the relation between us. Silence, at such a time, is itself capable of bearing the burden of truth, for it is "filled" silence in which the "I" and "Thou" hear each other "speaking" out of the fullness of their respective beings, and there is sharing unspeakable. The act, the decision, not the word, bespeaks the love and fidelity in which each lives for the other. It is the act and decision which alone is the true answer to another's unspoken need. "The really responsible men are those who can withstand the thousandfold questing glance of individual lives, who give true answer to the trembling mouths that time after time demand from them decision."[56]

Community means the enhancement and transformation of every sorrow and joy. We suffer more intensely because we widen the range of our responsibility for the other, taking up into our lives the pain and agony of the "Thou." Our sensitivity to the "Thou" insures that we will be placed under tribute to his afflictions. But we also find transmutation of our sorrows, not by their elimination, but because we stand with the other in them. The shared burden becomes itself the realization of community—and again a partial response to the love which suffers with and for the world. In a similar way every happiness and joy is lifted up into a new dimension. The everyday pleasures become shared pleasures which permit the participation of others in a full-bodied way. Humor flourishes at its most robust and sharpest. No longer the sniggering complacency of one who laughs "at" another and thereby establishes his own superiority. Now the wit which does not wound, no matter how pointed, because it is held within the bond of mutual esteem and affection. Only in community may we utter the most outrageous nonsense or ply another with jokes at his expense, because only there is the backlog of common appreciations strong enough to withstand fully without injury, only there is the freedom for the repartee which links persons together even when to the outsider it treads on dangerous ground.

Personal community is mutual fulfillment, but it can never turn in upon itself, so long as it is seen in the light of God's will to community. Personal community is not a private group, a closed society holding itself aloof from the common run of mankind. It is to be held as a response to God's love, and therefore must be open, open to Him and to the world insofar as finitude and our sinfulness permit. Community on the "I-Thou" level is subject to the even more far-reaching community which God wills for all men. Though we have but intimations of this more extensive community in this world, we look forward to a realization of it which transcends our earthly history and are invigorated by the prospect.

Personal community has buried in it the factor of mutuality.

Where there is mutuality of some kind at the heart of community, there is presupposed an element of equality of status. To have mutuality we must also have persons who are sufficiently alike in some regard so that communion can take place between them. Each must serve the other, but each can serve the other only if in some respects there is common intellectual, moral, and spiritual ground. The other's good becomes mine, as does mine, his. This is the ethic of reciprocity, the ethic of the Golden Rule, and this ethic has its halting point, the place where reciprocity is impossible. So the rule is not the maximum which Christian faith settles for in human relations. It sees a Cross, not simply a rule, no matter how sensitively this rule be worked out in personal community. The Cross is the evidence of a love which does not take its orders from consequences but pours itself out with a daring and courage drawn from the divine itself. The Cross is the evidence of a love which gives itself not on the basis of a calculated return but because it is its nature to be outgoing, catching within its scope those who in any human measure of judgment have forfeited the possibility of entering into community.

What of those persons who by force of circumstances beyond their control, insanity, cultural isolation, crippling physical and mental disease, or senility, have lost the capacity for response to personal community? What of those who by some dogged perversity of will stand off in rebellious isolation from their fellows or from God's mercy? And what of those who enter into associations with others only to secure for themselves some private advantage, those who play at "community" and make of it a travesty and a tool? The demoniac and the adulterous woman, the grasping Zacheus and the Pharisee, the Prodigal Son and the woman with her flask of precious ointment, the false prophets and the Jezebels, Pontius Pilate and the high priests—what do such as these know of community or love? They are the hindrances, the threats, the enemies to community. They are not its agents. They do not live, apart from faith, as those who have the least concern for love. And so long as mutuality, reciprocity, or justice be taken as the last word of faith for human conduct, they will remain outside the depth of community in any sense except that of society in general.

Yet faith is created by a love which brought it forth from the depth of unworthiness and claimed it for itself. It remembers that before it was capable of love, love acted. It remembers the power of God's love in creation, and in Christ who died on our behalf while we were yet unborn, while we were yet ignorant, while we were yet sinners. It remembers that by our existence in sin we crucify God's love anew daily. It remembers that in the strength of God's patient love and power we are daily renewed and lifted in hope. If then, by faith, we see ourselves created, judged, and redeemed by God's love in Christ, we cannot reject those who obstruct in the highest degree God's will to community. In them we but see ourselves, not as though we were forever past the point of becoming the Judases, the Pilates, the Pharisees or adulterers, but as those to whom betrayal, ruthlessness, smug self-righteousness, and lecherous thoughts are no strangers. We are the dull of mind and spirit; we are the stunted cripples and, for aught we know, will be the decrepit, senile, useless ones which fill up so large a part of the stage of human history. Yet Christian love is not flung widespread simply because we identify ourselves with the evildoers and the faltering, the rebels and conformists, the aged and ignorant. Nor does Christian love take its start from the thought that we, in comparison with these, have been "lucky" or especially favored. Insofar as we love those who cannot or will not return our love, we love by the measure of God's love to all men, not by the measure of their responsiveness or worthiness to be loved. Luther admitted "that a good man is more worthy to be loved than a bad one, and that we are naturally more drawn to him." He went on to add, "but true love is independent of such external considerations, and it seeks out primarily not those who are most attractive, but those who are most in need."[57] And in such love there is no place for condescension and self-congratulation. In their need, God speaks to faith, seeking the response of love.[58]

Love, therefore, steps out beyond what we have hitherto described as community. It seeks a community of reconciliation. It wishes to bridge the gap between persons; it yearns to repair the torn fabric of humanity in the light of the higher possibility of community. Yet love has to take the first step, not with the guarantee that community will be established, but because God so loved the world. For this reason, Christian love has an air of carelessness and rashness about it. It acts because of the unspeakable "carelessness" with which God speaks in love to the depth of any person. So love steps over barriers which would keep it out and, if nothing more, stands with those on the other side in their frustration and tragedy. It cannot force its own acceptance; it can only act forthrightly but with due sensitivity to the other person's rights. It may take up unto itself the anguish, guilt, loneliness, and shame of the neighbor, even when held at arm's length by the other. It bears the enmity and abuse of those who treat it as an interloper or are afraid of its audacity and the simplicity of its hope. It offers reconciliation, but it is not a "trick" by which the unique value of the other is engulfed in an ocean of wallowing sentiment. It serves without hope of return. It does not ponder on its own sublimity and superiority, nor does it heal its wounds with self-pity. It is love so deeply interwoven with the existence of the agent that it does not rise to self-conscious endeavor and contemplation. It simply goes about its task, the meeting of this person in need, with all the resources at its disposal. "Love suffers long, and is kind; envieth not . . . is not puffed up . . . seeketh not its own, is not provoked, taketh not account of evil . . . beareth all things."[59] And at last, it never fails, not because it always bridges the gap, wins the recalcitrant one, or heals the broken in mind and body, but because it is unquenchable and inexhaustible. It is God's gift, not our achievement. It is His love that never fails, not ours.

Upon this love is founded the supreme community, the communion of each with the other, of each with his Lord. It is of this community the church of Christ speaks; it is this community by which she is judged and in this community she is fulfilled as the church triumphant.[60] When she fails to open herself to the "spirit which bloweth where it listeth" she hardens into dogmatism and repels men by her coldness and rigidity. When she proposes that in herself she contains the full depth of community, her divisions rise up to call her "liar." When she shrilly castigates the evils of the world outside her doors, rather than indict the worldliness within, she becomes a nagging nuisance.[61] When she assumes the prerogatives of God Himself, making herself the dictator of men's salvation by her "possession" of creeds, sacraments, and "right" orders of worship, she succeeds only in appearing silly to the world. When she attaches herself to the fortunes of a state or a culture, she throws away her birthright and limply follows on after the decisions and acts of those who at a given time hold the centers of power. When she is not obedient to God's will to community, she becomes a monstrosity because she does not offer hope, but a new religious burden to be borne by those who have not the courage and wit to challenge her, and who instead settle for what they believe to be peace and security.[62]

Yet in the measure that the church takes seriously the love whereby she is created and renewed, she is the agent of community in the world. As she opens herself toward the world, "accepts the unacceptable," struggles for the weak and unjustly treated, sympathetically participates in the woes and joys of humanity, calls to account the mighty in the name of a higher justice, and offers herself as the place where divine mercy and righteousness may become incarnate, she finds she has not succumbed to the "world" but borne a faithful witness to her God. In the faith in which she exists and out of which she acts, her obedience turns toward community—the community which is itself ever open to God's love and criticism. When such love appears, then faith heralds its power with the cry of Paul: "I am sure that neither death, nor life, nor angels, nor principalities, nor things present, nor things to come, nor powers, nor height, nor depth, nor anything else in all creation will be able to separate us from the love of God in Christ Jesus, our Lord."

Notes

PREFACE

1. Henry Adams, *The Education of Henry Adams,* Boston, Houghton Mifflin Co., 1918, p. 451.

CHAPTER I. PRIMAL FAITH AND RADICAL FAITH

1. Cf. H. Höffding, *La Philosophie de Bergson,* Paris, Alcan, 1916, pp. 160-61.
2. W. Shakespeare, *Julius Caesar,* Act I, Scene 2; cf. K. Heim, *Christian Faith and Natural Science,* London, Student Christian Movement Press, Ltd., 1953, pp. 35 ff.
3. H. N. Wieman goes so far as to suggest that faith has its source in the human body itself. "The body so reacts that one is coerced to be aware that one is sustained. . . ." That vague "Something" which sustains may later be clarified into knowledge, but its reality "will not let him go and he knows that it will not, no matter how much he may cultivate his doubts." *Encyclopedia of Religion,* New York, The Philosophical Library, 1945, pp. 270-71. Dr. Wieman has struck upon a fundamental character of "primal faith"; however, I think this form of faith cannot be reduced entirely to bodily function. One depends no less completely upon psychological factors. B. Meland, in a similar vein, states, "Faith roots in the will to live; thus in its elemental form, it is hardly distinguishable from a biological attachment to life." *Faith and Culture,* New York, Oxford University Press, 1953, p. 63. I would suggest that faith, even at this rudimentary level, includes enacted "assent" as well as blind "attachment."
4. Note T. M. Greene's distinction between "initial" and "resultant" faith. *Religious Perspectives in College Teaching,* H. W. Fairchild (ed.), New York, Ronald Press, 1952, pp. 123 ff.
5. Cf. E. Brunner, *The Christian Doctrine of Creation and Redemption,* Philadelphia, The Westminster Press, 1952, p. 152.
6. Cf. F. N. Heinemann, "Belief, the Mother of Philosophy," *Hibbert Journal,* October, 1955, pp. 70 ff.
7. Cf. Gabriel Marcel, *The Philosophy of Existence,* London, The Harvill Press, 1948, pp. 8 ff.
8. W. E. Hocking, *The Meaning of God in Human Experience,* New Haven, Yale University Press, 1923, pp. 235-36.

9. K. Jaspers, *Tragedy Is Not Enough*, Boston, The Beacon Press, 1952, p. 41.

10. D. Bonhoeffer, *Ethics*, Eberhard Bettige (ed.), New York, The Macmillan Company, 1955, p. 123.

11. C. A. Bennett, *The Dilemma of Religious Knowledge*, New Haven, Yale University Press, 1931, p. 117.

12. Cf. E. Frank, *Philosophical Understanding and Religious Truth*, New York, Oxford University Press, 1945, pp. 9 ff.

13. Quoted by William Barrett, "What Is Existentialism?" *Partisan Review Series*, no. 2, 1947, pp. 23 ff.

14. P. Tillich, *The Shaking of the Foundations*, London, Student Christian Movement Press, Ltd., 1949, p. 169.

15. John S. Whale, *Christian Doctrine*, Cambridge, Cambridge University Press, 1952, p. 174.

16. C. E. Raven, "Experience and Interpretation," Second Series, *Gifford Lectures*, 1952, Cambridge, Cambridge University Press, 1953, pp. 24-25.

17. Quoted by K. Jaspers, *Reason and Anti-Reason in Our Time*, London, Student Christian Movement Press, Ltd., 1952, p. 55.

Chapter II. Some Misunderstandings of Faith

1. W. Lippmann, *Preface to Morals*, New York, The Macmillan Company, 1929, p. 60.

2. "It is acting a preposterous part to endeavour to produce sound faith in the Scriptures by disputations. . . . The Word will never gain credit in the hearts of men till it be conformed by the internal testimony of the Spirit," wrote John Calvin. Quoted by G. E. Wright, *The Challenge of Israel's Faith*, Chicago, The University of Chicago Press, 1944, p. 12.

3. G. Marcel, *The Mystery of Being*, Vol. II, *Faith and Reality*, London, The Harvill Press, 1951, p. 76.

4. Quoted by D. G. M. Patrick, *Pascal and Kierkegaard*, London, The Lutterworth Press, 1947, Vol. I, p. 32.

5. P. H. Waddell denies this tension and sees such faith as a form of credulity—a belief in the impossible. "This idea, however inconsistent, that faith implies doubt has clung to religious thought . . . the element of uncertainty is estimated as an increase of the virtue of trust, and the notion of venturing all on the unseen is supposed to give heroic self-sacrifice to the religious consciousness." *Essays on Faith*, Edinburgh and London, William Blackwood and Sons, 1903, pp. 152-53; cf. M. Holmes Hartshorne, "Faith without Doubt Is Dead," in *Theology Today*, April, 1956, pp. 63 ff.

6. Hebrews 11:1. Italics my own.

7. G. Aulén, *The Faith of the Christian Church*, Philadelphia, The

Muhlenburg Press, 1948, p. 325.

8. Quoted by W. Pauck, *The Heritage of the Reformation*, Boston, The Beacon Press, 1950, p. 20, (Luther's *Works*, Weimar Edition, 10, XII, 228, 15). Cf. also H. Martin, *Puritanism and Richard Baxter*, London, Student Christian Movement Press, Ltd., 1954, p. 129.

9. Cf. R. Bultmann, *Essays*, London, Student Christian Movement Press, Ltd., 1955, p. 303. Cf. also Ignatius von Döllinger's comment on papal infallibility: "Papal infallibility was in early times a matter of opinion, never of doctrine; and what a gulf there is between an opinion and an article of faith." *Conversations of Dr. Döllinger*, recorded by Louise von Kobell (English translation by Katherine Gould), London, Richard Bentley and Sons, 1892, p. 16.

10. Unfortunately, Bishop Stephen Neill erroneously assumes that criticism of creedalism is a sign of naïve individualism or liberalism. He fails to discriminate between community and institutionalism and therefore dismisses criticism of creeds in a facile manner. The tension between church as community and church as institution should never be lost sight of, even in the heat of enthusiasm for ecumenicity. Cf. Stephen Neill, *Christian Faith Today*, Baltimore, Pelican Books, 1955, pp. 171-72.

11. I John 4:23.

12. Vss. 9-11.

13. V. J. Bourke, *Ethics*, New York, The Macmillan Company, 1951, p. 462.

14. *Ibid.*, p. 470. Cf. also A. C. Pegis (ed.), *Basic Writings of Saint Thomas Aquinas, Summa Theologica* II, 2, Question 2, Articles 7 and 8, New York, Random House, 1944, Vol. II, pp. 1083-86.

15. Cf. Paul Tillich's statement: "The burden He [Christ] wants to take from us is the burden of religion." *The Shaking of the Foundations*, London, Student Christian Movement Press, Ltd., 1949, p. 95.

16. James 2:19.

17. "Preface to St. Paul's Epistle to the Romans," quoted in H. E. Fosdick, *Great Voices of the Reformation*, New York, Random House, 1952, p. 121.

18. C. S. Lewis points the moral of this position in the advice he has the senior devil give to the younger one. He counsels, "Keep your victims' gaze upon their feelings, not on God. Where they meant to ask Him for charity, let them instead start trying to manufacture charitable feelings for themselves. . . . Where they meant to pray for courage, let them be really trying to feel brave. . . . Teach them to estimate the value of each prayer by their successes in producing the desired feeling; and never let them suspect how much success or failure of that kind depends on whether they are well or ill,

fresh or tired at the moment." *The Screwtape Letters,* New York, The Macmillan Company, 1956, pp. 25-26.

19. Cf. Bourke, *op. cit.,* p. 461.

20. Aquinas, *op. cit.,* pp. 1096, 1098.

21. *Ibid.,* p. 1079.

22. M. Buber, *The Eclipse of God,* New York, Harper & Brothers, 1952.

23. Cf. Robert L. Patterson, *The Conception of God in the Philosophy of Aquinas,* London, George Allen and Unwin, Ltd., 1933, pp. 119 ff.; also pp. 181, 216, 223.

24. Cf. J. Baillie, *The Idea of Revelation in Recent Thought,* New York, Columbia University Press, 1956, p. 28. H. R. Niebuhr, *The Meaning of Revelation,* New York, The Macmillan Company, 1941; E. Brunner, *Revelation and Reason,* Philadelphia, The Westminster Press, 1946.

25. P. Tillich, *op. cit.,* pp. 116-17. Italics in text. Cf. also C. A. Bennett, *A Study of Mysticism,* New Haven, Yale University Press, 1923. "The first requirement for becoming truthful . . . is a grasp upon truthfulness as a universal. The virtue cannot be acquired piecemeal, by the learning of particular acts or special rules. . . ." The person "should first grasp the universal idea of truthfulness as a disposition of will, or spirit or principle of interpretation to be brought to bear upon particular instances." pp. 48-49.

26. P. A. Bertocci, *Introduction to the Philosophy of Religion,* Englewood Cliffs, Prentice-Hall, Inc., 1951, pp. 66, 82.

27. Of such definitions Waddell wrote, "Faith is not a blind and feeble venture, which by degrees you manage to prop and establish; nor is it the statement of a doubtful proposition, which by degrees you guarantee as more and more complete, and to which you add other subsidiary propositions as necessity arises." *Op. cit.,* pp. 6-7.

28. Dorothy Emmet, *Philosophy and Faith,* London, Student Christian Movement Press, Ltd., 1936, pp. 88-90.

29. Cf. Miguel de Unamuno, *The Tragic Sense of Life,* translated by J. E. Crawford Fletcher, New York, The Macmillan Company, 1921, p. 184.

30. E. Brunner, *Man in Revolt,* Philadelphia, The Westminster Press, 1947, p. 248.

31. Cf. *ibid.,* p. 43; also E. P. Dickie, *God Is Light,* London, Hodder and Stoughton, 1954, p. 132.

32. The syllabus of Dr. Werner Heisenberg's Gifford Lectures, delivered at St. Andrews University (1955-56) concludes with these suggestive words: "It has certainly been the pride of natural science since the beginning of rationalism to describe and to understand Nature without using the concept of God, and we do not want to give up any of the achievements of this period. But in modern atomic

physics we have learned how cautious we should be in omitting essential concepts just because they lead to inconsistencies. We have been forced to recognize the essential limitations of any language by which we try to find our way through the existing world." p. 16.

33. Cf. John A. Hutchison, *Faith, Reason, and Existence,* New York, Oxford University Press, 1956, p. 108.

34. P. T. Forsyth, *The Person and Place of Jesus Christ,* London, Independent Press, 6th ed. 1948, p. 200.

35. W. Temple, *Nature, Man and God,* New York, The Macmillan Company, 1935, p. 322.

CHAPTER III. FAITH AND CHRIST

1. Cf. D. M. Baillie, *God Was in Christ,* New York, Charles Scribner's Sons, 1948, pp. 73-74.

2. With vast erudition Karl Barth tortures the evidence for a Virgin Birth into a dogma for the Christian faith, but his efforts, though impressive, remain totally unconvincing. Cf. K. Barth, *Church Dogmatics,* Vol. I, Part 2, "The Doctrine of the Word of God" (translated by G. T. Thomson and Harold Knight), Edinburgh, T. and T. Clark, 1956, pp. 172 ff.

3. John's gospel evidences embarrassment about a baptism of Jesus by an "inferior" personage. No actual baptism is reported, but examination of 1:29 ff. reveals the shadowy form of the Synoptic tradition. Matthew and Luke also deal with the baptism in characteristic ways, suggesting that they were uneasy about it. The "brute datum" of historical fact, however, shows through.

4. Mark 1:4, Luke 3:3.

5. Mark 1:15.

6. I Corinthians 15:5 is the earliest recorded account we have of the Resurrection. It purports to be a recital of the accepted tradition of the Christian church. Comparison of the Resurrection stories shows them to be quite incompatible as to time and place. No one account, so far as the four gospels show, held the field uncontested. What is more important, however, is that the Resurrection is treated as a series of appearances covering a substantial period of time. All attest to the supreme conviction that Christ is triumphantly alive.

7. W. A. Whitehouse, *Christian Faith and the Scientific Attitude,* New York, The Philosophical Library, 1952, p. 72.

8. D. M. Baillie, *op. cit.,* p. 50. Cf. J. Macquarrie, *An Existentialist Theology,* New York, The Macmillan Company, 1955, pp. 170-71, 180.

9. P. T. Forsyth, *The Person and Place of Jesus Christ,* London, Independent Press, 1948, p. 44.

10. Cf. E. Brunner, *The Christian Doctrine of Creation and Redemption,*

Philadelphia, The Wesminster Press, 1952, p. 257.

11. Cf. P. Tillich, *Systematic Theology,* Chicago, The University of Chicago Press, 1951, Vol. I, pp. 118 ff.

12. J. Knox, *Christ and Lord,* Chicago, Willett Clark and Co., 1945, p. 50.

13. B. Anderson, *Rediscovering the Bible,* New York, Association Press, 1951, p. 189.

14. "Faith consists in the fact that henceforth man knows that his life, his very self, is a gift from God, not a life which is striving after God." E. Brunner, *The Divine Imperative,* New York, The Macmillan Company, 1937, p. 77.

15. Mark 2:17.

16. J. Calvin, *Institutes of the Christian Religion,* Philadelphia, The Wesminster Press, 1936, Vol. II. Book III, Chap. xix, par. 5, p. 80.

17. The "imitation of Christ" motif, familiar in medieval piety, does not bulk large in the gospels, if it is to be discovered at all. This may be due to two factors: (a) Jesus does not appear to have used it as a sign of discipleship; (b) the earliest Christians regarded him as the unique revelation of God, and as such simply impossible of imitation. The Synoptics picture Jesus calling men "to follow," "to repent," "to listen or obey"; the Fourth Gospel has him demanding belief, obedience, and love. The mystical writer of the Fourth Gospel calls for unity with Christ, not imitation of him.

18. Matthew 7:21.

19. As evidence for this statement the following considerations are offered. In Mark's gospel, Jesus repudiates the term "good" as applied to himself because God alone is good. He wrestles with temptation after the baptism, an act which in itself raises grave doubts about any identification of Christ and God. He prays to God and in Gethsemane cries out for the removal of the cup of death, "yet not what I will, but what thou wilt." He utters the strange words of dereliction from the cross. He never appropriates the designation of Creator. While there is the consciousness of a profoundly intimate communion with the Father, he and the Father do not merge. Even the Gospel of John finds the exalted Christ saying, "He who believes in me, believes not in me but in him who sent me." It is remarkable that when this gospel dares to identify Christ and God, the idea of duality is still present: "My Father, *who has given them to me,* is greater than all, and no one is able to snatch them out of the Father's hand. I and the Father are one." (John 10:29-30.) The entire doctrine of the Resurrection hinges upon this duality of Jesus and God, for it is not God who dies and raises Himself, but this unique personage Christ who dies and is raised by God. So the Petrine sermon of Acts has it: "be it known to you all . . . that by

the name of Jesus Christ of Nazareth, whom you crucified, whom God raised from the dead, by him this man is standing before you well." (Acts 4:10.) See also A. W. Wainwright, "The Confession 'Jesus is God' in the New Testament," *Scottish Journal of Theology,* Sept. 1957, pp. 274 ff.

20. Cf. Acts 4:10.
21. Matthew 5:45. J. Klausner finds in this expression a dangerous notion suggesting that Jesus' God is indifferent to the moral order. He argues that this doctrine would spell the ruin of historic Judaism and was therefore rightly repudiated by it. I am doubtful of the interpretation placed upon Jesus' words by Klausner. J. Klausner, *Jesus of Nazareth,* New York, The Macmillan Company, 1926, pp. 379-80.
22. II Corinthians 5:18-19a.
23. Cf. Matthew 9:1-13; especially 11:18-19; Luke 7:36-50. Luke 15 incorporates three parables on the theme of the acceptance of "sinners," their lostness and redemption.
24. Mark 3:34b-35.
25. Cf. P. Tillich, *The Shaking of the Foundations,* London, Student Christian Movement Press, Ltd., 1949, pp. 161-62.
26. Quoted in Hugh Martin, *Richard Baxter and Puritanism,* London, Student Christian Movement Press, Ltd., 1954, p. 136.
27. D. M. Baillie, *op. cit.,* p. 184.
28. Romans 5:8.
29. J. Macquarrie argues that the Resurrection must have been an "objective-historical event," not merely an "existential-historical" event, according to his reading of Bultmann. However, he is no more successful than others before him in delineating what constituted the "objective-historical event," upon which the "existential" meaning is founded. He covers his retreat by saying "that Christ appeared to his disciples after his death—in what way we do not presume to say, nor do we think it needful to inquire." J. Macquarrie, *op. cit.,* p. 187; cf. H. D. A. Major, T. W. Manson, and C. J. Wright, *The Mission and Message of Jesus,* New York, E. P. Dutton and Co., 1948, pp. 215 ff.
30. Cf. Richard R. Niebuhr, *Resurrection and Historical Reason,* New York, Charles Scribner's Sons, 1957, pp. 172-81.
31. J. Knox, *op. cit.,* p. 62.

CHAPTER IV. FAITH AND GOD, ITS ULTIMATE OBJECT

1. Cf. E. J. F. Arndt (ed.), *The Heritage of the Reformation,* New York, R. R. Smith, 1950, p. 107.
2. Cf. C. A. Bennett, *The Dilemma of Religious Knowledge,* New Haven, Yale University Press, 1931, pp. 109-10.

3. E. Brunner, *The Divine-Human Encounter,* Philadelphia, The West-minster Press, 1943, pp. 21, 22-23, 41.

4. *Ibid.,* p. 86.

5. Will Herberg, *Judaism and Modern Man,* New York, Farrar, Straus, and Young, 1951, p. 60.

6. M. Buber, *The Eclipse of God,* (translated by Maurice S. Friedman et al.) New York, Harper & Brothers, 1952, p. 91; *I-Thou,* (translated by Ronald Gregor Smith), Edinburgh, T. and T. Clark, 1937, p. 112. For fuller treatment of Buber's position, see P. Pfuetze, *The Social Self,* New York, Bookman Associates, 1953; Leslie Paul, *The Meaning of Human Existence,* London, Faber and Faber Ltd., n.d., pp. 148 ff.; James Brown, *Subject and Object in Modern Theology,* London, Student Christian Movement Press, Ltd., 1955, chap. V.

7. A. Farrer, *The Glass of Vision,* Westminster, Dacre Press, 1948, pp. 7-8. Cf. also E. P. Dickie's comment on Farrar's statement in *God Is Light,* London, Hodder and Stoughton, 1954, pp. 148 ff.

8. A. N. Whitehead, *Religion in the Making,* Cambridge, Cambridge University Press, 1930, pp. 51-52. Cf. P. Tillich, *The Courage to Be,* New Haven, Yale University Press, 1952, pp. 182 ff.

9. Quoted by E. P. Dickie, *op. cit.,* pp. 33-34. Cf. R. Otto, *The Idea of the Holy,* New York, Oxford University Press, 1925, Appendix V, pp. 201 ff. Cf. W. M. Horton, *Christian Theology,* New York, Harper & Brothers, 1955, pp. 105-10.

10. The Biblical record shows how impossible it is to maintain either the third-person or second-person categories when referring to God. It is also instructive to note how often the power, anger, and spirit of God are represented by "impersonal" notions: e.g., "ruach" as a power without personal form; *to pneuma* as in John 3:8—"The wind [spirit] blows where it wills, and you hear the sound of it, but you do not know whence it comes or whither it goes; so it is with everyone who is born of the Spirit"; Elijah's experience in I Kings 19:11— "And behold, the Lord passed by, and a great and strong wind rent the mountains, and broke in pieces the rocks before the Lord, but the Lord was not in the wind . . ." i.e., He transcended the natural force, yet it accompanied His coming; other media of God's power, such as fire, cloud, burning bush, and even the ambiguous term "word" (*logos*) are typical efforts to represent the numinous quality of the divine.

11. Cf. J. Brown *op. cit.,* pp. 150-51.

12. K. Jaspers, *Reason and Anti-Reason in Our Time,* London, Student Christian Movement Press, Ltd., 1952, p. 35. Friedrich Gogarten claims that the subject-object pattern is "inextricably linked with the Cartesian view of the world and reality." *Demythologizing and History* (translated by H. H. Smith), New York, Charles Scribner's

Sons, 1955, p. 50. All that can be successfully argued is that Descartes offered one interpretation of the subject-object pattern. However, he did not discover or invent the relation; his treatment of it need not be accepted as normative, and therefore the subject-object pattern is not "inextricably linked" with Cartesian perspectives.

13. Cf. H. A. Hodges, *The Philosophy of Wilhelm Dilthey,* London, Routledge and Kegan Paul, Ltd., 1952, pp. 56 ff.

14. Buber's position calls for more extended analysis and criticism than we can develop here. For criticisms see J. Brown, *op. cit.,* pp. 186 ff. Pfuetze (*op. cit.*) is critical of Buber at certain points but heralds prematurely the I-Thou relation as having undercut the subject-object relation. Friedman's excellent exposition is marred by an overly protective attitude toward Buber. He tends to construe all criticism as misunderstanding. He, like Pfuetze, finds Buber has cut underneath all subject-object distinctions. Cf. Maurice S. Friedman, *Martin Buber, the Life of Dialogue,* London, Routledge and Kegan Paul, Ltd., 1955, pp. 163 ff.

15. Even Barth, who holds God as personal subject, makes much of the "objectivity" of God. "God speaks, he makes demands, he promises, he acts, he is angry, he is gracious. Remove the objectivity of this 'he' and faith as love, trust, and obedience also collapses." Quoted in Otto Weber, *Karl Barth's Church Dogmatics* (Arthur C. Cochrane, translator) Philadelphia, The Westminster Press, 1953, p. 74. Cf. also J. Brown, *op. cit.,* p. 191.

16. John Burnaby uses the figure of battle effectively in connection with faith when he writes: "Faith is the sacramentum, the oath of enlistment in which the individual accepts allegiance to God's sovereignty; but if His Kingdom were already come in the fullness of its power, there would be no warfare to wage . . . and just because the fight is real, and no bloodless, predetermined manoeuvre, he must quit himself like a man, hoping not to save his soul, but to do his part in winning the victory." *Amor Dei,* London, Hodder and Stoughton, 1947, p. 317.

17. Quoted by W. E. Hocking, *The Meaning of God in Human Experience,* New Haven, Yale University Press, 1923, p. 239.

18. "Faith in God . . . is never easy for men. Instead, it comes normally in times of genuine and profound disturbance in the self. Faith and crisis go hand in hand." A. Outler, *Psychotherapy and the Christian Message,* New York, Harper & Brothers, 1954, p. 176.

19. Jeremiah 20:7-9; 15:18.

20. Mark 4:36b.

21. As Whitehead remarked, "It belongs to the depth of the religious spirit to have felt forsaken, even by God." To which it must be added that neither Jeremiah nor Jesus was forsaken; He is present

to them as the Void or Enemy, and this gives greater poignancy to their struggles. A. N. Whitehead, *op. cit.*, p. 9.

22. Cf. H. R. Niebuhr, *The Meaning of Revelation,* New York, The Macmillan Company, 1941, pp. 152-53.

23. Cf. Gabriel Marcel, *The Mystery of Being,* Vol. II, *Faith and Reality,* London, The Harvill Press, 1951, pp. 133-34.

24. John Flavel, the English Puritan, saw acceptance as a deeper element of faith than assent and assurance: "A true believer may 'walk in darkness, and see no light.'. . . Many a man must be a believer before he knows himself to be so. The direct act of faith is before the reflex act, so that the justifying act of faith lies neither in assent nor in assurance. . . . But acceptance which saith, I take Christ in all his offices to be mine, this fits it exactly. . . ." Quoted by John Baillie, *The Idea of Revelation in Recent Thought,* New York, Columbia University Press, 1956, p. 89.

25. P. T. Forsyth, *The Person and Place of Jesus Christ,* London, Independent Press, 1948, pp. 197-98.

26. Cf. P. Tillich, *The Courage to Be,* New Haven, Yale University Press, 1952, pp. 172-73.

27. "The basic possibilities for man are that he can be estranged from himself (inauthentic existence) or at one with himself (authentic existence) and it is only his relation to God in faith that can give him a right relation to himself, or make him at one with himself." J. Macquarrie, *An Existentialist Theology,* New York, The Macmillan Company, 1955, p. 202.

28. H. R. Niebuhr, *op. cit.*, p. 185.

29. Cf. Alec R. Vidler, *Christian Belief,* London, Student Christian Movement Press, Ltd., 1950, p. 92.

30. Cf. G. Marcel, *op. cit.*, p. 134.

31. Cf. Luke 17:7-10.

32. G. Aulén, *The Faith of the Christian Church,* Philadelphia, The Muhlenburg Press, 1948, p. 25. Cf. also J. Burnaby, *op. cit.*, p. 34.

33. Cf. Nicolas Berdyaev, *Freedom and the Spirit,* London, Geoffrey Bles, The Centenary Press, 1948, 4th ed., p. 119. W. M. Horton is so bold as to state that "true Christian freedom is a synonym for the salvation of the soul." *Our Christian Faith,* Boston, The Pilgrim Press, 1945, p. 74.

34. Galatians 5:1.

35. II Corinthians 3:17.

36. Robert Bretall (ed.), *A Kierkegaard Anthology,* Princeton, Princeton University Press, 1946, p. 428.

37. E. Brunner, *Christianity and Civilization,* New York, Charles Scribner's Sons, 1948, Vol. I, pp. 131-32.

38. "The first charge on a true and positive theology is regard for the

freedom of God. That is the only source and condition of man's freedom. The prime condition of human freedom is a free God, and such faith as seeks first his freedom, and has all other things added unto it." P. T. Forsyth, *op. cit.*, p. 87.

39. Abraham Heschel, "The Dimension of Holiness," in *The Journal of Religion*, vol. 23, no. 2, 1943, p. 110.

40. Jonathan Edwards, *Works*, (1817 edition) Vol. IV, p. 285.

41. Cf. Thomas S. Kepler, *The Fellowship of the Saints*, Nashville, Abingdon Press, 1948, pp. 123-24.

42. W. J. Oates (ed.) *Basic Writings of Saint Augustine*, New York, Random House, 1948, Vol. I, p. 342.

43. Jude, 24-25.

Chapter V. Faith and the Ethical Question

1. Cf. Romans 10:5-9

2. Classifications of ethical theories remain the despair of moral philosophers, though the divergencies should not be exaggerated. Cf. C. D. Broad, *Five Types of Ethical Thinking*, New York, Harcourt, Brace and Company, 1939; N. H. G. Robinson, *The Claim of Morality*, London, Victor Gollancz, 1952, pp. 260 ff.; T. E. Hill, *Contemporary Ethical Theories*, New York, The Macmillan Company, 1950; and many more.

3. W. D. Falk, *Ethics*, January, 1956, p. 131.

4. "Christian ethics," writes George F. Thomas, "was never intended to be an 'ethical theory' which would solve in a systematic and comprehensive manner all the problems of morality, as it was not intended to be a new code of laws specifying what men should or should not do in every kind of situation." *Christian Ethics and Moral Philosophy*, New York, Charles Scribner's Sons, 1955, p. 380.

5. This position is succinctly stated by W. D. Falk. "Morality, as we understand it, is logically independent of religious authority. Morality . . . still stands or falls on the possibility of arriving at such a conviction [of the right or good] independently of any authority." *Op. cit.*, p. 128. It is a nice question how any aspect of human experience can have anything but relative independence or autonomy in a unitary world.

6. H. R. Niebuhr, in *The Heritage of the Reformation*, E. J. F. Arndt (ed.), New York, R. R. Smith, 1950, p. 223.

7. Cf. R. Bretall, *A Kierkegaard Anthology*, Princeton, Princeton University Press, 1946, pp. 197-98.

8. C. A. Bennett, *The Dilemma of Religious Knowledge*, New Haven, Yale University Press, 1946, p. 31.

9. Cf. H. J. Paton, *The Categorical Imperative*, Chicago, The University of Chicago Press, 1948, p. 196; Thomas, *op. cit.*, p. 376.

10. Cf. John Hick, *Faith and Knowledge,* Ithaca, Cornell University Press, 1957. There is, of course, knowledge about faith, but this is not to argue that faith itself is a form of knowledge.

11. P. H. Waddell, *Essays on Faith,* Edinburgh and London, William Blackwood and Sons, 1903, p. 204.

12. J. Baillie, *Our Knowledge of God,* New York, Oxford University Press, 1939, p. 33.

13. Cf. K. Jaspers, *Reason and Anti-Reason in Our Time,* London, Student Christian Movement Press, Ltd., 1952, p. 65.

14. R. Niebuhr, *The Self and the Dramas of History,* New York, Charles Scribner's Sons, 1955, p. 12.

15. See Kierkegaard's analysis of this problem in *The Sickness Unto Death,* New York, Doubleday and Co., 1954, pp. 223 ff.

16. Cf. J. V. Langmead Casserley, *Morals and Man in the Social Sciences,* London, Longmans, Green and Co., 1951, pp. 76, 77.

17. D. Bonhoeffer, *Ethics,* Eberhard Bettige (ed.), New York, The Macmillan Company, 1955, p. 235.

18. C. A. Bennett, *A Study of Mysticism,* New Haven, Yale University Press, 1923, p. 169.

19. P. Tillich, *Love, Power and Justice,* New York, Oxford University Press, 1954, pp. 76-77. Cf. also K. Barth, *Church Dogmatics,* G. Bromley and T. F. Torrance (eds.), Edinburgh, T. and T. Clark, 1956, Vol. I, Part 2, pp. 384 ff.

20. Cf. J. Bennett, "The Christian Response to Social Revolution," in *The Ecumenical Review,* vol. 9, no. 1, 1956, p. 6.

21. Cf. Edward Cahn, *The Moral Decision,* Bloomington, Indiana University Press, 1956, pp. 38-39.

22. Bonhoeffer went so far as to say that God's commandment leaves no room for application or interpretation. It leaves room only for obedience or disobedience. ". . . If God's commandment is not clear, definite, and concrete to the last detail, then it is not God's commandment." D. Bonhoeffer, *op. cit.,* p. 245. This is dangerous doctrine, inasmuch as it comes close to admitting that men can read off fully and explicitly the will of God in a specific situation. Hence, faith, with its element of doubt and tension, and moral action, which always is carried out in a trembling respect to God himself, are nullified. He has, in sum, erected criteria for the will of God, a course of action which evokes the most serious misgivings.

23. E. Brunner, *The Divine Imperative* (translated by O. Wyon), New York, The Macmillan Company, 1937, p. 70. Cf. also R. L. Calhoun, *God and the Common Life,* New York, Charles Scribner's Sons, 1935, p. 44.

24. Cf. H. D. Lewis, *Morals and Revelation,* London, George Allen and Unwin, Ltd., 1951, pp. 126 ff.

25. I. Kant, *Critique of Practical Reason and Other Works on the Theory of Ethics* (translated by T. K. Abbott), London, Longmans, Green and Co., 3rd ed., 1883, pp. 355-56.
26. N. H. G. Robinson, *Faith and Duty*, New York, Harper & Brothers, 1950, p. 11.
27. "The attempt at self-recovery through any deliberate effort of will such as assuring ourselves that we ought to see value in the things that have unaccountably lost it, is hopeless. . . ." C. A. Bennett, *op. cit.*, p. 138; cf. K. Jaspers, *Reason and Existenz*, London, Routledge and Kegan Paul, 1956, pp. 122-23.
28. *Basic Writings of St. Augustine*, W. J. Oates (ed.), New York, Random House, 1948, p. 503.
29. His alternative formulation is "temperance is love keeping itself entire and incorrupt for God; fortitude is love bearing everything readily for the sake of God; justice is love serving God only, and therefore ruling well all else, as subject to man; prudence is love making a right distinction between what helps it toward God and what might burden it." *Ibid.*, pp. 331-32.
30. H. D. Lewis, *op. cit.*, p. 148.
31. E. P. Dickie, *God Is Light*, London, Hodder and Stoughton, 1954, p. 75.
32. Dr. Paul Weiss boldly states: "Religion has nothing to do with ethics except to provide it with a new context." *Moral Principles of Action*, Ruth N. Anshen (ed.), New York, Harper & Brothers, 1952, p. 220.
33. P. Tillich, *op. cit.*, p. 72.
34. Cf. Geddes MacGregor, *Les Frontières de la Moralité et de la Religion*, Paris, Aubier, éditions Montaigne, 1952, pp. 89, 177 ff.
35. I have not attempted to review the whole problem of the relation of Christian faith and ethics. For further comments on this problem cf. G. Thomas, *op. cit.*; Paul Ramsey, *Basic Christian Ethics*, New York, Charles Scribner's Sons, 1950; W. G. DeBurgh, *From Morality to Religion*, London, Macdonald and Evans, 1938; Bernhard Häring, *Das Heilige und Das Gute*, München, Erich Wewel Verlag, 1950; Theodor Steinbüchel, *Religion und Moral im Lichte Personaler Christlicher Existenz*, Frankfurt am Main, Verlag Josef Knecht, 1951.
36. Cf. Otto Kirn, *Grundriss der Theologische Ethik*, Leipzig, A. Sechert, 1906, pp. 2-3, 23-24.
37. A. E. Taylor, *The Faith of a Moralist*, New York, The Macmillan Company, (reprint 1951), Vol. II, p. 68; also E. P. Dickie, *op. cit.*, p. 78; cf. A. N. Whitehead, *Science and the Modern World*, New York, The Macmillan Company, 1925, p. 224.
38. D. M. Baillie, *God Was in Christ*, New York, Charles Scribner's Sons, 1948, p. 116.

CHAPTER VI. FAITH AND COMMUNITY

1. Martin Buber, *Images of Good and Evil*, London, Routledge and Kegan Paul, 1952, p. 83.
2. Cf. Otto Weber, *Karl Barth's Church Dogmatics, an Introductory Report* (A. C. Cochrane, translator), Philadelphia, The Westminster Press, 1953, p. 105.
3. Matthew 22:37-40.
4. Cf. Romans 5:8-10.
5. I John 4:19.
6. Cf. P. Lehman, "The Foundation and Pattern of Christian Behavior," in *Christian Faith and Social Action*, J. Hutchison (ed.), New York, Charles Scribner's Sons, 1953. Cf. also E. Brunner, *The Divine Imperative* (O. Wyon, translator), New York, The Macmillan Company, 1937, pp. 92 ff.
7. Quoted in H. E. Fosdick, *Voices of the Reformation*, New York, Random House, 1952, p. 93. Cf. P. Ramsey, *Basic Christian Ethics*, New York, Charles Scribner's Sons, 1950, p. 136.
8. "When it is . . . admitted that the best actions of all are not strictly obligatory, it is time to give up saying that obligation is the defining feature of the moral life and therefore the central idea of ethics." T. E. Jessop, *Law and Love*, London, The Epworth Press, 1948, p. 58.
9. Cf. E. P. Dickie, *The Obedience of a Christian Man*, London, Student Christian Movement Press, Ltd., 1944, p. 26.
10. D. Bonhoeffer, *Ethics*, New York, The Macmillan Company, 1955, p. 327. P. Lehman speaks to the same point: "Since it is simply a fact, that the ethical cannot be detached from the real situation, the increasingly accurate knowledge of this situation is a necessary element of ethical action." *Op. cit.*, p. 106.
11. Cf. T. E. Jessop, *op. cit.*, pp. 102-3.
12. Cf. J. C. Bennett, *Christian Ethics and Social Policy*, New York, Charles Scribner's Sons, 1946, pp. 77 ff.; cf. also E. L. Long, Jr., *Conscience and Compromise*, Philadelphia, The Westminster Press, 1954, pp. 80-81.
13. J. C. Bennett, *op. cit.*, p. 77.
14. It has been a favorite charge of non-Christian moralists to point out that Christianity has repeatedly confused its tactics with divine revelation, thereby perpetrating and sanctioning moral outrages in the name of the most high. Unfortunately, Christian faith must agree with this criticism. (Cf. Errol E. Harris, "Objectivity and Reason," in *Philosophy*, January, 1956, p. 57.) However, it also points out that (a) it is not only religious ethics, including Christian ethics, that falls into this trap of absolutizing the finite—compare the French Revolution with its slogan of "Reason" etc.—and (b) there

is an alternative way of formulating Christian moral responsibility, represented by our own position.

15. Cf. J. C. Bennett, *op. cit.*; H. F. Reissig, "Aid and Trade," in *Social Action*, vol. 24, no. 7, pp. 16, 17; Victor Obenhaus, *The Responsible Christian*, Chicago, The University of Chicago Press, 1957, pp. 104-105, 169; Albert T. Rasmussen, *Christian Social Ethics*, Englewood Cliffs, Prentice-Hall, Inc., 1956, chap. 6.

16. Donald Baillie remarked that "Christianity is the religion of community" and thought it possible that a whole theology might be developed from that standpoint. However, he also warned against the danger of making "community" into a "blessed word." *The Coracle*, January, 1951, p. 10.

17. R. L. Calhoun, "Christian Vocations on the College Campus," in *The Christian Scholar*, Supplement Issue, Autumn, 1954, pp. 270-71.

18. D. D. Williams, *God's Grace and Man's Hope*, New York, Harper & Brothers, 1949, p. 151.

19. N. Ferré, *Christian Faith and Higher Education*, New York, Harper & Brothers, 1954, p. 81.

20. E. Brunner, *Man in Revolt*, London, The Lutterworth Press, 1939, p. 289.

21. R. Bultmann, *Essays*, London, Student Christian Movement Press, Ltd., 1955, pp. 291 ff. The severe criticism passed upon Bultmann's treatment of community based on religion, made by John Macquarrie, is not warranted. Cf. J. Macquarrie, *An Existentialist Theology*, New York, The Macmillan Company, 1955, p. 224.

22. E. Brunner, *Man in Revolt*, p. 106.

23. Cf. K. Jaspers, *Reason and Existenz*, London, Routledge and Kegan Paul, 1956, p. 84.

24. R. Bultmann, *op. cit.*, p. 303; E. Brunner, *Man in Revolt*, p. 290.

25. Cf. E. Brunner, *Man in Revolt*. Cf. also Jonathan Edwards, *Treatise Concerning True Virtue*, where this theme is worked out in metaphysical terms.

26. Cf. H. R. Niebuhr, *Christ and Culture*, New York, Harper & Brothers, 1951, chap. 1.

27. Leslie Hunter, *The Seed and the Fruit*, London, Student Christian Movement Press, Ltd., 1953, p. 35.

28. I have in mind the speculations of such men as Lloyd Morgan, Henri Bergson, A. N. Whitehead, J. C. Smuts, H. N. Wieman, C. Hartshorne, and others.

29. C. A. Bennett referred to "the superb indifference of Nature to all human ends and distinctions, an indifference which does not seem to shut us out from a kind of communion with her" but which "enables one to set these ends and distinctions in a proper perspec-

tive." *A Study of Mysticism*, New Haven, Yale University Press, 1923, pp. 181-82.

30. H. R. Niebuhr, *The Meaning of Revelation*, New York, The Macmillan Company, 1941, pp. 152, 167.

31. Cf. J. Calvin, *Institutes of the Christian Religion*, Philadelphia, The Westminster Press, 1936, Book IV, chap. xiv, par. 18.

32. Bultmann betrays a tendency both to biblicism and to anthropocentricism when he states, "There is no sense in speaking of the revelations of God in nature; for nature does not exhibit what is essential for God-omnipotence." *Op. cit.*, p. 100. If he means that nature does not clearly witness to God as creator, judge, and redeemer, apart from Christ, there is no debate. If, on the other hand, he in sum denies God's sovereignty by refusing to admit that God has and does meet man through nature (e.g., as in passages of the Old Testament, some of Jesus' parables and statements), the proper answer to his statement is "nonsense." Wherever God meets men there is revelation; whatever He is Lord over, inclusive of nature, can be and is the medium of revelation. God continues to shake man's complacency in his control over nature, not only by Christ, but by the fact of death, which itself, in one aspect, is "natural." In man's essential dependence on and participation in nature, he is reminded that he is not self-sufficient. This kind of insight seems to come only in its unique and irreplaceable form through nature. Of course, nature does not reveal God's omnipotence. Not even Christ does that! It is even doubtful whether such a term as "omnipotence" is meaningful in reference to deity. Cf. E. P. Dickie, *God Is Light*, New York, Charles Scribner's Sons, 1954, pp. 3, 4.

33. C. Michalson, "Between Nature and God," in *Journal of Religion*, October, 1955, p. 237.

34. Cf. M. Friedman's careful treatment of this whole point, with differing conclusions from my own, in his *Martin Buber, the Life of Dialogue*, London, Routledge and Kegan Paul, Ltd., 1955, pp. 169 ff. I find support from Buber's critics at this juncture. Cf. James Brown, *Subject and Object in Modern Theology*, London, Student Christian Movement Press, Ltd., 1955

35. Paul Tillich treats this theme movingly in his sermon "Nature Mourns a Lost Good," in *The Shaking of the Foundations*, London, Student Christian Movement Press, Ltd., 1949. The painting "Tierschicksale" by Franz Marc (1913) will repay appreciative study in this connection (Basel, Kunstmuseum).

36. G. Marcel, *The Philosophy of Existence*, London, The Harvill Press (Changing World Series no. 2), 1948, pp. 30-31.

37. Isaiah 11:6 (University of Chicago translation).

38. Romans 8:19-23. For the meaning of the term *ktisis* ("creation")

see Kittel, *Theologisches Wörterbuch zum neuen Testament,* Stuttgart, 1938, Band III, pp. 1027 ff.

39. Revelation 21:11. The Christian apocalyptic seems to believe that nature is so far lost that it can only be replaced rather than "redeemed." However, in the vision of a new heaven and earth, it is still held that a kind of nature will participate in the glory of salvation. The sea, however, will be no more!

40. Colossians 1:20. Cf. Alan Galloway, *The Cosmic Christ,* London, Nisbet and Co., Ltd., 1951.

41. H. H. Rowley has pointed up this conception in his comments on the Old Testament conception of the individual and the community. "While he [the Israelite] is liable to suffer for the common sins, or for the sins of other individuals, he also receives a rich inheritance from those who have gone before and from his contemporaries, and from both he may receive great blessings. If he shares ills he has done nothing to deserve, he also receives blessings he has not merited." "Individual and Community," in *Theology Today,* January, 1956, p. 503.

42. Cf. Kenneth Boulding, *The Organizational Revolution,* New York, Harper & Brothers, 1953, p. 78. Cf. also T. E. Jessop, *op. cit.,* pp. 12-13.

43. Cf. Ian Henderson, *Can Two Walk Together?* London, Nisbet and Co., Ltd., 1948, p. 125. Cf. also P. Tillich, *Love, Power, and Justice,* New York, Oxford University Press, 1954, pp. 62, 68.

44. Hope Nicholson, "The Mind Has Mountains," in *The Observer,* Sunday, March 11, 1956. It is only fair to put alongside this testimony on behalf of the "impersonal" that found in M. Friedman, *op. cit.,* chap. 21. Here is pointed out the possible significance of the "I-Thou" relation in psychiatric treatment.

45. E. Brunner, *Man in Revolt,* p. 294.

46. Cf. M. Friedman, *op. cit.,* p. 97.

47. Walt Whitman, "Song of the Open Road," in *Leaves of Grass,* New York, Doubleday, Doran and Co., Inc., 1940, p. 13.

48. Cf. M. Friedman, *op. cit.,* p. 45.

49. E. Brunner, *Man in Revolt,* p. 290.

50. Cf. H. A. Hodges, *The Philosophy of Wilhelm Dilthey,* London, Routledge and Kegan Paul, Ltd. 1952, p. 10. (International Library of Sociology and Social Reconstruction). Cf. also A. N. Whitehead, "The world is a scene of solitariness in community. . . . The individuality of entities is just as important as their community." *Religion in the Making,* Cambridge, Cambridge University Press, 1930, p. 76.

51. R. Bultmann, *op. cit.,* p. 301. Of course, this does not mean that only persons with this acute understanding of the faith relation are able

to enter into community with each other. All we are concerned to suggest is that for the man of faith this initial situation of "isolation" establishes and protects the unique worth and individuality of man in community. He is not, as it were, swallowed up. Cf. Ronald Grimsley, *Existentialist Thought,* Cardiff, University of Wales Press, 1955, p. 165.

52. Cf. E. Brunner, *Man in Revolt,* pp. 282-88.
53. D. Bonhoeffer, *op. cit.,* pp. 145, 146.
54. One of Bultmann's definitions of human community seems as adequate as any, though it fails to encompass the richness of community. Human community is "that community in which man finds himself devoting himself to his fellow-men. Genuinely human community is found only between men who reveal themselves to one another in their true selves, and are themselves for each other and through each other." R. Bultmann, *op. cit.,* p. 292. Cf. also M. Friedman, *op. cit.,* pp. 43 ff. G. Gusdorf, *La Parole,* Paris, Presses Universitaires de France, 1956, pp. 57-86.
55. M. Buber, *Between Man and Man,* London, Routledge and Kegan Paul, Ltd., 1947, p. 114.
56. M. Friedman, *op. cit.,* p. 43. Or as Buber puts it: "I call a great character one who by his actions and attitudes satisfies the claim of situations out of deep readiness to respond with his whole life, and in such a way that the sum of his actions and attitudes expresses at the same time the unity of his being in its willingness to accept responsibility." M. Buber, *Between Man and Man,* p. 114.
57. Cf. P. Watson, *Let God Be God,* Philadelphia, The Muhlenburg Press, 1950, p. 107.
58. Cf. T. E. Jessop, *op. cit.,* p. 32.
59. I Corinthians 13:4 ff.
60. "By foundation and destiny" the Church "is designed to express in the world the ethos of man's interrelatedness and openness for man." P. Lehman, *op. cit.,* p. 107.
61. "Christianity is less an exposure of obvious badness than an indictment of obvious goodness." T. E. Jessop, *op. cit.,* p. 4.
62. Cf. R. Gregor Smith, "The Church and the World," in *The Student World,* no. 3, 1954, p. 235 (Geneva). Cf. also E. Brunner, *Man in Revolt,* p. 295.

Index